Soviet Poets and Poetry

Soviet
Poets
and Poetry

By

ALEXANDER KAUN

Essay Index Reprint Series

BOOKS FOR LIBRARIES PRESS, INC.
FREEPORT, NEW YORK

891.71
K215l
122859

Preface

APRIL 23, 1932, is an important date in the history of Soviet letters. On that day the Central Committee of the ruling Party issued a resolution which is considered by writers of the Soviet Union as a declaration of independence. By dissolving the RAPP (Russian Association of Proletarian Writers) and allied groups the resolution set aside a factor that had terrorized individual authors and crippled all creative activity. The policy of regimentation was denounced, and an end was put to the division of artists into the privileged and sacrosanct "proletarians" and the suspected and persecuted "fellow travelers" and other "class enemies." Henceforth all qualified authors who accepted the basic principles of the existing order were to be eligible to a single Union of Writers, recognized and protected by the State. The hegemony of any one class or group or school would not be tolerated. The one tendency officially approved, and adhered to by virtually all writers, was designated as Socialist Realism. Though this term predicates a Marxian-Socialist point of view, it is broad and elastic enough to be all-embracing for Soviet artists.

This revolutionizing measure is typical of the zigzag policies of the Bolsheviks, who have on numerous occasions shown their readiness to discard, under the pressure of circumstances, one way or method for its opposite. To realize the meaning of the 1932 "revolution," we must survey, however cursorily, the field of literary currents and tendencies in the Russian republic. The literatures of national minorities have, on the whole, shared the fate of Russian literature; they are, however, left out of this account.

This essay is intended as part of a larger work in progress, a survey of all Soviet literature, from 1917 to our own day. Some of the theories and tendencies discussed herein may have a closer relation to prose than to poetry, but in a certain measure they are all relevant to literature as a whole. The space allotted to each current depends on its relative importance at the time it was in evidence. The same proportion I have applied (with no claim to objectivity) to individual poets. Dates are given, except when unavailable:

Unless otherwise indicated, the translations quoted are by me. In rendering poetry I have made no effort at correct versification; my aim has been to convey the spirit and substance of the original and, when possible, its rhythm.

For the sake of brevity I have used the word "Party" to indicate the Communist Party. Since this is the only party in existence in the Soviet Union, there is no need of any qualification. For the same purpose I have employed abridged combinations of easily understandable terms; e.g., sovbourgeois for Soviet bourgeois.

I wish to pay my respects to the predecessor of my survey, *Popular Poetry in Soviet Russia,* by my colleague, Professor George Z. Patrick. Copious and varied illustrations make that book invaluable for the student of recent Russian poetry. The purpose of Professor Patrick's book, and its scope, are quite different, however, from those of my essay.

To the Board of Editors of the University of California Publications in Modern Philology, particularly to Professor George R. Noyes, I am greatly beholden for helpful criticism and numerous suggestions for the improvement of my effort.

A complete list of the materials used for this essay would be impressive, but hardly interesting for those who do not read Russian. Poets of note I have found available in more or less complete editions. Among these are: Demyan Bedny; Khlebnikov; Mayakovsky; Aseyev; Yesenin; Selvinsky; Bezymensky; Kirsanov; Tvardovsky; Kryukova, and a few others. To David Burlyuk I am grateful for a number of publications containing his verse and reproductions of his paintings. For other poets I have consulted various symposia, anthologies, and periodicals that have appeared since the revolution. Contemporary discussions, polemics, and critiques

I have found in abundance in such periodicals as *Pechat i revolutsia, Krasnaya nov, Zvezda, Novy mir, Oktyabr, Literaturny kritic, Literatura i marksism, Literaturnaya gazeta,* as well as in numerous journals published by groups and grouplets of passing fame and ephemeral duration. The incomplete *Sovietskaya entsyklopedia* and *Literaturnaya entsyklopedia,* and Vladislavlev's bibliographic guides have been helpful. A fairly comprehensive though lamentably prejudiced "Chronicle of Soviet Literature, 1917–1932" was published in *Literaturny kritik,* 1–12 of 1937 and 1 of 1938.

Among the books of reference I have used I should mention: *Literaturnyie manifesty ot simvolizma k oktyabryu* (1929), manifestoes and declarations compiled by N. Brodsky and others; V. Lvov-Rogachevsky's *Ocherki proletarskoy literatury* (1927), a vivid journalistic sketch of proletarian literary efforts; *Proletariat i literatura* (1925), a collection of articles for and against proletarian literature by divergent critics, among them Lelevich, Lunacharsky, Klara Zetkin, Ivan Maisky, Trotsky, Voronsky; books of literary criticism by these and others (Polonsky, Peter Kogan, Lezhnev, Gorbachev, Kubikov, Lebedev-Polyansky, Averbach), whose pertinence stops with the 1920's; Lvov-Rogachevsky's *Imaginisty* (1921) gives a brief account of early Moscow imagists; N. Gorlov's *Futurism i revolutsia* (1924), A. Kruchonykh's *15 let russkavo futurizma* (1928), V. Kamensky's *Put' entuziasta* (1931), and several recent (1939–1941) monographs and memoirs about Mayakovsky contain some factual data on futurism; for formalistic tendencies I sought information in critical studies by V. Shklovsky, B. Eichenbaum, Y. Tynyanov, R. Yakobson; a rather fair Marxian appraisal of formalism appeared in I. Vinogradov's *Borba za stil* (posthumous edition 1937), and in P. Medvedev's *Formalism i formalisty* (1934).

Acknowledgment is due to the *American Review of the Soviet Union,* the *Slavonic Year Book, Soviet Literature, Art, Music* (London), and *New Directions* (1941), in which certain parts of this essay have previously been published.

A. K.

Contents

Chapter I ◇ Introduction

THE OCTOBER, 1917, hurricane meant a clean sweep of old forms of Russian life. It is now a truism to state that the revolution not only transformed political, social, and economic relations, but profoundly affected religion, science, and art as well. The thoroughness and the speed with which the destruction of the old took place, may not have been intentional. One may suppose that Lenin and his aides were prepared for the gradational tempo of an evolutionary process. What accelerated and deepened this process was the refusal of the old to give way to the new, or to merge with it, and its sullen resistance, both passive and active. War Communism, with its drastic leveling, was the direct consequence of counterrevolutionary risings and foreign intervention. By the same token, the "sabotage of the intelligentsia," as the Bolsheviks branded the refusal of sundry experts to coöperate with them, caused a swift change in the intellectual and artistic aspects of the country. The change was sharply felt in the plastic arts and in the arts of verbal expression—that is to say, literature and the stage.

As a matter of fact, the literary morning after the Bolshevik Revolution was pretty drab. One might even question the very existence of literature, in any event of prose, during the first four years of the new order. Nearly all the big names were lined up on the opposite side of the barricade, literally and figuratively. For generations the intelligentsia, and most conspicuously the writers, had championed the people and the revolution. Now that both had triumphed, but had proved neither gentle nor genteel, their former champions felt disappointed and cheated. Once safely abroad, they loudly renounced their former idols, and such spokesmen as the dainty poets Zinaida Hippius (b. 1869) and Ivan Bunin (b. 1870) proclaimed undying hatred for the pig-snouted people and holy vengeance against their leaders, the Cains and Judases. Those who, willingly or perforce, stayed at home, where they grumbled secretly or sulked in silence, formed the so-called "inner emigration." Even Maxim Gorky (1868–1936) fought the Bolsheviks for nearly a year, until his newspaper was silenced; thereafter, becoming reconciled to the regime, he engaged for years in cultural rather than literary work, except for sporadic reminiscences. Such writers as Veresayev (b. 1867), Serafimovich (b. 1863), Sergeyev-Tsensky (b. 1867), were not to recover their voices for some time to come. Alexey Tolstoy (b. 1882) was an emigrant, in danger of joining the band of sterile Jeremiahs; his change of heart and return home took place later. Other names flared up now and then in short-lived periodicals and miscellanies, ineffectual heat lightnings.

This paralysis of belles-lettres, whatever its psychological causes, had also a definite economic explanation: the shortage of paper and printing facilities under conditions of civil war, intervention, and blockade. Most of the printed output had an official stamp; only a thin trickle was allowed for items not directly connected with the immediate needs of a state engaged in a desperate fight against inner and foreign enemies, and against the very elements of nature.

Poetry fared otherwise, being one of the few muses not silenced by cannon. In vitality and popularity it was second only to the even more robust darling of the revolution, the theater, but poetry reached a larger audience. The brevity and pithiness of a poem appealed to a nation on the march. A poem could be published without a heavy tax on the insufficient paper supply and the overworked printing press, or could circulate even without the benefit of typography. Poetry made itself felt most intensely at the lowest ebb of the country's economic life. During the nightmarish winters of civil and interventionist wars, the starving and freezing citizens were entertained by a swarm of minstrels, ranging from the outmoded realists and symbolists to such postsymbolists as acmeists (known also as adamists), futurists, imagists, constructivists, such ephemerals as biocosmists, form-librists, expressionists, neoclassicists, luminists, nothingists (*nichevoki*),[1] not to mention sundry proletarian groups.

While war raged on some sixteen fronts, large audiences in military and civilian garb packed the unheated coffee houses of Petrograd, Moscow, and other large centers. It was not so much the sugarless carrot tea that drew the crowds, as the far more stimulating fare offered by writers who were unable to reach the public by means of the printed word. Celebrities and unknown striplings grappled with one another, and recited their latest poems jotted down on scraps of wrapping paper or the backs of ancient invoices, or from memory. Some of the best poetry of the period received its first hearing at these café gatherings. Ballads, marching songs, and jingles were welcomed by the fighting armies as spiritual ammunition for the raw, ill-shod, and poorly equipped recruits. By way of analogy: in the past the icon had triumphed in religious art over the mosaic and the fresco by virtue of its portability, laconism, and comparative cheapness. On a smaller scale—as the clientele was more limited—poetry supplied a similar popular demand for spiritual food.

Another fact should be noted. Unlike the prose writers, the poets overwhelmingly "accepted" the revolution. Not more than half a dozen of the leading poets definitely rejected the new order, and of these only Gumilyov (1886–1921) represented the young and the vital.[2] The rest had had their say, had lost their flexibility. At their best they could be expected to be repetitious and venom-spitting, when abroad (Balmont [b. 1867], Hippius, Bunin), or

---

[1] The nothingists, who signified a goodly portion of this sound and fury, advocated extreme refinement, subtilization of poetic forms, images, rhythm, "instrumentation, colophons": "Refinement will reduce art to zero, will destroy it, will lead it into nothing, bring it to nothing. Our aim is the refinement of poetic productions in the name of nothing." They proclaimed the slogan:

"Write nothing!   Say nothing!
Read nothing!   Print nothing!"

[2] In 1921 he was implicated in a conspiracy and shot.

repetitious and moping, when "inner emigrants" (Sologub [1863–1927]). With these exceptions, Russia's poets attuned themselves to the changed regime. Not that all of them followed the example of Valery Bryusov (1873–1924), who subscribed to the Bolshevik platform immediately after the October uprising. Whatever their individual views, doubts, and misgivings, the poets regarded the revolution as an elemental transformation of life, which they were impelled to reflect. From the days of Pushkin (1799–1837), the Russian poet had seen himself as life's "echo."[3] The revolution failed to dumfound him, as it did other artists of the pen. "Listen to the music of the revolution!" was the call and challenge of Alexander Blok (1880–1921) in those critical hours. The poets did listen, and, in the measure of their receptivity and responsiveness, they sang. As the chorus was bewilderingly multiple, let us consider at least the leading voices, shortly before 1917 and thereafter.

---

[3] Pushkin's *Echo* (1831) runs thus:

"Whether a beast roars in the dense forest,   You harken to the rumble of thunders
Whether a horn blares, or thunder claps,   And to the voice of storm and billows,
Or a maiden sings beyond the hill,   And to the cries of village shepherds,
To every sound   And you send an answer;
Your response in the void air   But for you there's no reply . . .
Promptly comes forth.   Such are you too, poet!"

Chapter II ❖ On the Eve

STARTING in the eighteen-nineties as decadents and rebels, frequently bent on shocking the respectable elements of society (Bryusov's one-line "poem,"

> *O zakroy tvoi blednyie nogi*
> O cover thy pallid legs,

was typical of the *épater* phase), the Russian symbolists became virtually the dominant school of poetry by 1910. One hesitates to apply the word "school" to so heterogeneous a group. The distinct personalities were united by rather negative penchants, in aesthetics away from realism, in ideology away from democratic and populist notions, and especially from the growing Marxian materialism. As the movement spread and lost the cohesion of fellow iconoclasts, the differences within it grew in intensity. The religious mystics, Merezhkovsky (1866–1941), Hippius, Vyacheslav Ivanov (b. 1866) differed from one another only slightly less than from the satanic solipsist, Sologub, or from the dainty yet Mozart-like clear, depraved yet innocent Kuzmin (b. 1877), or from the brilliant B's—the mellifluous pagan, Balmont, the austere Lithuanian, Baltrushaitis (b. 1873), the classically cold, erotic Bryusov, the anthroposophic word symphonist, Bely (1880–1934), and the misty clairvoyant, Blok. Their pantheon housed Dionysos and Christ, Epicurus and Nietzsche, Vladimir Solovyov (1853–1900) and Rudolph Steiner.

Whatever their philosophical diversity, the symbolists possessed such common traits as erudition, cosmopolitism, aesthetic fastidiousness, and a subtle use of words and sounds to suggest overtones, secondary meanings. At home in classical and modern world literature, they flaunted their catholicity in mottoes and slogans.

Goethe's "Alles Vergängliche ist nur ein Gleichniss" became a threadbare phrase.[1]

Like Western symbolists, the Russian group derived chiefly from the French. Hence the frequent references to Baudelaire's *correspondances*,[2] the emphasis on Mallarmé's dictum that the artist must suggest rather than name,[3] the preoccupation with the musical quality of words, according to Verlaine.[4] Their avowed allegiance to foreign *maîtres;* their fondness for remote and exotic themes, and the "other-meaningness" of their vocabulary lent the symbolists both fascination and obscurity.

Regarded at first as iconoclasts and eccentrics, the symbolists gradually gained recognition and leadership, above all in poetry and literary theory. The "civic" note which had prevailed in Russian literature left little room for aesthetics. Above everything else the reader had expected guidance, answers to life's urgent questions, that outlet for public opinion which in civilized countries is provided by freely functioning political parties, parliamentary institutions, newspapers, and public meetings. For the same reason the critic had evaluated a literary production primarily for the message it conveyed. The symbolists forced a revision of this attitude. Their early exaggerations and extravagances, the usual features of a new movement, could not hide their splendid array of talent and scholarship, which soon began to exert influence. The obvious excellences of symbolist prose and verse could not help affecting both readers and critics. The literary craftsmanship was raised to a higher level and, what was more significant, to a state

---

[1] Some symbolists borrowed another shibboleth from the second part of *Faust,* "das Ewig-Weibliche," but for the most part they regarded this conception through the mystic prism of Vladimir Solovyov, who lent his Eternal Woman the attributes of Σοφία. Both Bely and Blok began as disciples of Solovyov. Blok's early cycle of *Verses to the Unknown Lady* is imbued with yearning for femininity of the Solovyov hue.

[2] "Les parfums, les couleurs et les sons se répondent."

[3] "Nommer un objet, c'est supprimer les trois quarts de la jouissance du poème qui est faite du bonheur de deviner peu à peu: le suggérer, voilà le rêve."

[4] "De le musique avant toute chose." *Cf.* Bely: "Music ideally expresses symbols. Hence the symbol is always musical."

of independence and esoteric sovereignty. It was no longer possible to ignore form for the sake of contents: the symbolists, for all their precious formalism, have shown the basic interdependence of the two.

By 1910 the symbolist group had reached maturity and began to show signs of both stagnation and disintegration. The erstwhile iconoclasts had become respectable in their own traditionalism, ripe for the brand of "academicians" soon to be applied to them by their offspring. In their preoccupation with the magic of sounds and the mystery of symbols, they drifted farther and farther from reality into foggy narcissism. Leading symbolists meanwhile diverged ever more widely in their quests and tenets; poets of vision, such as Alexander Blok, who sensed the imminent social thunderstorm, fretted at the airlessness of their ivory tower. The younger poets rebelled against their masters. One of the rebel groups, the acmeists, demanded liberation from the mistiness of symbols, setting forth clarity and directness as poetic virtues. Their gifted leader, Gumilyov, declared their kinship with Shakespeare, Rabelais, Villon, and Gautier (foreigners, again, with the same French preponderance). Gumilyov wrote:

> Each one of these names is a cornerstone for the edifice of Acmeism. . . . Shakespeare has shown us man's inner world, Rabelais—our body and its delights, . . . Villon has told us of a life that is fully self-confident even though imbued with the knowledge of everything, of God and vice and death and immortality. Théophile Gautier has discovered garments of irreproachable forms, worthy of that life—in art. To combine these four elements is the dream which at the moment unites those who boldly call themselves acmeists.

Unlike the symbolists, who soared in a mystic Beyond and regarded their art as a liturgy, even as a theurgy (V. Ivanov; A. Bely), the acmeists underlined the nonesoteric quality of their craft in assuming the label of a Guild of Poets. Osip Mandelstam (b. 1891), one of their brilliant poets and theoreticians, advocated using words expertly and reverently, with the selective precision of a craftsman choosing his working material. Rejecting the verbal fancifulness of the symbolists, he employed with skill words of common speech, characteristically giving to his book of verse the title *Stone*. "We are introducing Gothic into word relations," he declared, "in the way Ba h brought it into music." Perhaps the most popular member of the group was Anna Akhmatova (b. 1888). She achieved poignant effectiveness by using everyday words and phrases, stark in their simplicity and transparency, to convey shades of emotion and tragedy.

FUTURISTS

The efflorescence of futurism gave a new impetus to the disintegration of the symbolists. The emergence of acmeism had signified not so much a complete break with the parent school as a secessionist variant within the family. Futurism, on the other hand, was launched as a revolt against all schools and traditions. To be sure, as nearly every new movement had done with regard to its predecessor, futurism used symbolism as a springboard for its further leap, though its protagonists would protest against the idea of their kinship with anything or anyone. For twenty-odd years the futurists carried on a noisy and vehement existence, splitting into branches and factions, generating imitators and epigoni, and exerting a patent influence on poetry and the other arts.

Like most nonrealist currents in Russia, futurism owed its inception to a foreign source. As early as 1910, Marinetti's *Manifesto* (1909) was echoed by the ego-futurists in St. Petersburg and the cubo-futurists in Moscow. What made the Italo-French futurism and its Russian variants kindred, aside from the tenuous bond of their tenets, was the *succès de scandale* they roused, and relished. Like Marinetti and his coterie, the Russians were not content with composing futurist poetry. They beat the drums of notoriety, campaigned and vociferated, tirelessly sought to *épater* the public by manifestoes, declarations, and personal appearances on the platform. In Moscow, futurist poets and painters amused the curious by painting their faces in rainbow colors and wearing yellow shirt-waists. As to ideas, they borrowed from Marinetti the revolt against stagnant traditionalism and authorities of the past, on the one hand, and, on the other, urbanism with its concomitant worship of dynamics, speed, and the machine.[5]

Russian imitativeness has long been noted and often deplored as a sign of lack of originality. Turgenev's Potugin, in *Smoke,* could not think of a single Russian invention save the samovar, and even that he regarded as a modification of a foreign product. From the time of Catherine II and Fonvizin, the aptitude of the quasi-Europeanized Russian for aping foreigners and borrowing a Western veneer has served as a theme for caricature and burlesque.

---

[5] Marinetti urged the need of new motives in art, the destruction of the old, the slow, the sentimental, the replacement of centaurs and angels by automobiles and airplanes. Thus:

"We had been listening to the emaciated prayer of the old canal and to the rattling bones of old palaces, with that verdant landscape of theirs, when lo, of a sudden, avid automobiles roared beneath our window. 'My friends,' I said, 'let us go. Let us move on. At last mythology and mystic ideals have been overcome and eclipsed. We shall presently attend the birth of a [mechanical] centaur and witness the flight of first angels.' "

For another sample of Marinetti's ideas and verbiage I shall cite a few excerpts from the eleven "commandments" regarded by Giuseppe d'Arrigo as "il fondamento del movimento futurista" (*Il poeta futurista Marinetti: sintesi della vita e dell'azione,* Roma, anno XV, pp. 23–24):

"We want to sing love of danger, the habitude for energy and daring. Courage, audacity, rebellion shall be essential elements of our poetry.... We want to exalt aggresive movement, febrile insomnia, the racing pace, the acrobat's somersault, the slap in the face and the blow of the fist (*lo schiaffo ed il pugno*).... Poetry must be conceived as a violent assault against unknown forces, to impel them to prostrate themselves before man."

"We assert that the magnificence of the world has been enriched by a new beauty: the beauty of speed.... A roaring automobile, which seems to whir across grape-shot, is more beautiful than the Victory of Samothrace."

The elasticity of Marinetti's dynamics, which ultimately brought him into the bosom of Mussolini's Fascism, may be seen in these additional fragments from the "commandments":

"We want to glorify war—only hygiene of the world, militarism, patriotism, the destructive gesture of liberators, beautiful ideas for which to die, and contempt for woman.

"We want to destroy museums, libraries, academies of all sorts, and to fight moralism, feminism, and all opportunistic and utilitarian vileness.

"We will sing the great throngs agitated by labor.... We will sing the many-colored and polyphonic tides of revolution in modern capitals. . . ."

One should bear in mind, however, that while it was natural for Russians, as late arrivals in history, to borrow from more advanced countries, they have not been mere copiers. Geographically and ethnically an amalgam of Asia and Europe, Russia has been able to absorb foreign elements and influences by recreating them and lending them a peculiar substance and form. Russians have borrowed copiously from the world treasure house of thought and art, and what they borrow they proceed to intensify, to further and deepen, to synthesize and thus render universal. Their painting and architecture are no less intimately Russian because of their Byzantine source, nor is the literary output of Pushkin and his successors unoriginal by reason of its indebtedness to Western Europe. German Romantic philosophy, especially its views on history, fathered Slavophilism, the arch-Russian doctrine of the last one hundred years. One may venture to suggest that, though based on Marxian theory, the Bolshevik regime has not been, and will certainly not develop into, a mere blueprint of society as conceived by Karl Marx. In the same way, the borrowed French slogans did not deprive Russian symbolist poetry of its original qualities. Nor did the influence of Marinetti and his group on the Russian futurists go beyond generalities and points of departure.

For one thing, neologisms and a new syntax, advocated by futurists of all lands, could not help betray the linguistic peculiarities of individual countries. Marinetti bestowed upon the new poet a "wireless imagination," which stood for "the absolute freedom of images and similes to be expressed by the liberated word, without any wires of syntax or any punctuation marks." The Russians practiced this "freedom" with a vengeance, making it the most conspicuous feature of their revolt against authority and tradition. As to the positive plank of Marinetti's platform, urbanism and modern machinery, its championship in backward prerevolutionary Russia appeared premature and artificial. For a short time this note sounded quite blatantly, then it gave room to more natural, native motifs.

Ego-Futurists.—The vulgarizer of the movement, and for a while the leader of the ego-futurists, was Igor Severyanin (b. 1887). Endowed with an extraordinary facility for coining new words, or rather for modifying and combining known terms, and gifted with a sense of rhythm and melody, Severyanin gained a swift though ephemeral popularity. The glitter of his verse and its genuine musical quality won for him the recognition of such serious poets as Sologub and Bryusov. Severyanin and his followers loudly espoused "all-powerful egoism," free from reticence and convention. "I, genius Igor Severyanin, I am screened omni-urbanly, I am ubi-cordially enthroned," is typical of this "I-I-I" poetry. He greets Bryusov "as one Great hails another Great," slaps him on the back as a "brother titan," and advises him that the two of them have "the realm of beauty in their hands." With "Ego-God" he is on familiar terms, and just as nonchalantly he proclaims: "Venus has given herself to me—and I am universally renowned!" The "ego" element was thus well taken care of, and as for the "futurity" side, Severyanin expressed it by means of non-Russian "exotics." He concocted gaudy words and phrases that savored of bars and boudoirs, and recited or rather chanted them quite effectively before enthusiastic middle-class audiences. These relished the saccharine verses, with their titillating rhythm and foreign words, and saw the acme of modernity, or futurity, in such phrases as "lilac ice cream," "pineapples in champagne, I am arrayed *à la* Spain," *"Garçon,* improvise a brilliant five-o'clock!"

The less gaudy, and less notorious, Severyanin is not undeserving of a place in modern poetry. The musical quality of his verse is evident even in translation, as the English reader may judge from the following two pieces, "And It Passed by the Seashore" and "A Russian Song," in the fine version[6] of Babette Deutsch and Avram Yarmolinsky.

---

[6] Included in *Modern Russian Poetry: An Anthology,* Harcourt, Brace and Co., 1921.

And It Passed by the Seashore

Poeza Mignonette

And it passed by the seashore, where the foam-laces flower,
Where the city barouches only rarely are seen. . . .
There the queen played her Chopin in the high palace tower,
And there, listening to Chopin, the young page loved the queen.

And what passed there was simple, and what passed there was charming:
The fair page cut the pomegranate as red as her dreams,
Then the queen gave him half thereof, with graces disarming,
She outwearied and loved him in sonata-sweet themes.

Then she gave herself stormily, till night shut her lashes.
Till the sunset the queen lay, there she slept as a slave. . . .
And it passed by the seashore where the turquoise wave washes,
Where sonatas are singing and where foam frets the wave.

A Russian Song

Lace and roses in the forest morning shine,
Shrewdly the small spider climbs his cobweb line.

Dews are diamonding and looming faery-bright.
What a golden air! What beauty! Oh, what light!

It is good to wander through the dawn-shot rye,
Good to see a bird, a toad, a dragon-fly;

Hear the sleepy crowing of the noisy cock,
And to laugh at echo, and to hear her mock.

Ah, I love in vain my morning voice to hurl,
Ah, off in the birches, but to glimpse a girl,

Glimpse, and leaning on the tangled fence, to chase
Dawn's unwilling shadows from her morning face.

Ah, to wake her from her half-surrendered sleep,
Tell her of my new-sprung dreams, that lift and leap,

Hug her trembling breasts that press against my heart,
Stir the morning in her, hear its pulses start.

The cheap popularity of Severyanin soon set him apart from any group. The ego-futurists themselves felt uncomfortable in his company, and disavowed him. Most of them went beyond the facile sweetishness of Severyanin; both in form and contents they tended to shock rather than flatter the average taste. I. V. Ignatyev, for instance, one of their pillars, acquired his reputation through a panegyrical poem to Onan. Vasilisk Gnedov in his booklet *Death to Art!* had a "Poem to the End" which consisted of a blank page. Ignoring other tricksters and shockers, we should mention Vadim Shershenevich (b. 1893), the cleverest member of the group. Some of his verses sound like deliberate parodies of Severyanin. One suspects him of holding his tongue in his cheek, as one reads such a poem of his as "L'Art poétique," wherein he counsels one to treat poems like "society ladies," to humor them with witticisms but to spare them the embarrassment of "hopeless drama," to rouge their cheeks and pencil "dreamily their dark-blue eyebrows," to dress them in *jupe-culottes* and have their hands braceleted with "aerial rhyme," finally to "misbehave with them amidst the halls of Academia."

In his less frivolous moments Shershenevich has the power of invoking pathos and drama. A sample of his verse, if only in a literal prose translation, may give one an idea of his talent:

> The crowd hummed like a trolley wire,
> The sky was concave like a lampshade.
> The moon shone through a cloud,
> Like a woman's foot in an openwork stocking.
> And in the bespattered square, amid fireworks
> Of allurements and phrases, ecstasies and poses,
> A nude woman drooped, sad and lusterless,
> Standing up on a bench, in gloves of roses.
> The crowd giggled, in laughter exchanging
> Cruel pain and reproaches—while up there,
> At her feet, crawled a lavender little girl,
> Tears, like rhymes, flowing down her cheeks.

Another sample:

> The year I've forgotten, but I recall it was Friday.
> Driving up to the entrance in a common hack,
> I bade the gray-haired concierge
> To let me up the lift to you: sixth floor.
> You, feverishly violet, from the window
> Saw me, and came out on the top landing.
> Alone I entered the lift, and pushing up the cable,
> Genial in advance, I removed my right glove.
> Lo, when the cable of the hoist already
> Shortened to the end, and I had reached the fourth,
> I could hear from above your insinuating song,
> From below another, sung by the devil.
> Suddenly it stopped, the finical lift.
> I was caught between two floors,
> And I tossed, and I sobbed, and I wept vexedly,
> A mouse in a mousetrap.
> Ever higher you receded through the roof,
> While the devil sang ever louder, ever brighter,
> Till I could hear only his song,
> And down I flew.

Vadim Shershenevich was extremely sensitive to contemporary moods and, while above imitation and plagiarism, he served as a weathercock, reflecting in his verses the vogue of the moment—now Balmont's Swinburnean melodiousness, now Blok's heartache for the Unknown Lady, now the macaronic gaudiness of the elegant, extravagant, and ever so gallant Igor Severyanin. He may therefore be regarded as a characteristic ego-futurist, just as in his subsequent stage of evolution he appeared as the legitimate spokesman of imagism. Shershenevich was both the poet and the theoretician of the movement. His "A Couple of Last Words" may be regarded as the mature expression of ego-futurism, or rather as a retrospective avowal of the group at its vanishing point. This statement is temptingly quotable, even though in translation its linguistic peculiarities are in large part lost.

Shershenevich demands in the name of modernity, or futurity, the liberation of words from the burden of meaning. "Free the words from their sense and contents, which have stuck like chewed paper about the word's pure image. The conversational word is as much related to the poetic word as a dead crow is related to an aeroplane. There is not, and should not be, any sense or contents in art." Yet in the next breath he proclaims the need of impregnating words with a futuristic content: "Learn to comprehend our automobilean words. The days of the current second are infused with *doping,* and are speeding at the rate of forty hours per second. The old poetry, laced in moonlight, barcaroles, trips on the lake, logic-affinity to Mr. Reason, with whom she has carried on an illicit affair, and to whom she has borne two rachitic children, naturalism and symbolism—this poetry has died from inanition." The past is rejected, with all its schools, for even the great poets of the past "had their feet hobbled by the narrow skirt of regular rhyme and meter." "We are too busy to imitate," he sneeringly advises the adherents of the past, and admonishes them to "smash the monocle of ages that has cut into the flesh." "Your today is an impostor, a reproduction of yesterday." The poetic muse has fled from Hellas, and has nailed a To Let sign on the gate of Parnassus. The muse has moved to the new electrified city, where romantic antiques are for sale at low prices, where "the frayed tassels of moonlight are sold out by the yard, and the jelly of clouds by the pound." The muse is no longer "in danger of spraining her ankle in a slipper with a French heel, for now she is not walking on foot but speeding in a motorcar, loudly shouting:

'Gentlemen! Look, the machine has transpierced each second with its scream. I blare off day after day with my siren. My arms stretch bridge-wise across the Atlantic Ocean. I am the reflection of everything: of the seething foam of wharves and foundries, the bellies of railroad stations, the flywheel of the sun-disk revolving across the teeth of clouds, locomotives losing on the run, professor-like, tufts of their smoke-hair and bristling the gray steam of their moustachios, of skyscrapers with the swollen abscesses of their balconies [*sic*]. And if you fail to understand my outcry, it is only because you are afraid of Today. Learn to value and comprehend the world's sole beauties: the beauty of form and the beauty of speed!' "

Cubo-Futurists.—The Moscow group of cubo-futurists differed from their St. Petersburg brethren in being more authen ically Russian and in using the collective "We" in place of the "I" of the "egos." They struck the keynote in their first declaration, with its suggestive title: "A Slap in the Face of Public Taste." This brief and pungent declaration may be quoted in full:

To those who read our New First Unexpected.

We alone are the *face of our Time.* Time's clarion blares forth in us, in our art of words.

The past is stifling. The Academy and Pushkin are more incomprehensible than hieroglyphs. Overboard from the steamship of modernity with Pushkin, Dostoyevsky, Tolstoy, and others, and others!

He who will not forget the *first* love, will not know the last. Who, then, is so gullible as to direct his last love to the perfumed lechery of Balmont? Can the audacious spirit of Today find therein its reflection? Who, then, is so craven as to hesitate in pulling the paper armor off the black frock-coat of warrior Bryusov? Are the dawns of unknown beauty thereon?

Wash your hands that are sticky with the filthy slime of books written by those innumerable Leonid Andreyevs.

A summer villa by the river, is all that's desired by these Maxim Gorkys, Kuprins, Bloks, Sologubs, Remizovs, Averchenkos, Chornys, Kuzmins, Bunins, and others, and others. Fate metes out such a reward to tailors.

From the height of skyscrapers we look down on their paltriness.

We command to honor the rights of poets:

1. To an enlargement of the poet's vocabulary by arbitrary and derivative words—neologisms.

2. To an insurmountable hatred for the language used previously.

3. With horror to thrust aside from their proud brows the wreath of cheap fame made out of your bathhouse brooms.

4. To stand firmly on the rock of the word "we" amid the sea of hisses and indignation.

If, for the time being, even our lines still retain the foul brands of your "common sense" and "good taste," across them already flutter the Heat-lightnings of a New Oncoming Beauty of the Self-Sufficient Word.

D. BURLYUK. A. KRUCHONYKH.
V. MAYAKOVSKY. V. KHLEBNIKOV.

Moscow. December, 1912.

The four signers of the declaration continued to give the tone to the movement, elaborating their views in subsequent statements. From the beginning the cubo-futurists had little in common with the Marinetti group, and, unlike the ego-futurists, they accentuated their native Russian traits. In fact, they claimed priority and independence, for as early as 1908 some of them made desultory attempts at futuristic painting and poetry, and, anticipating Marinetti, they called themselves *budetlyane,* a word coined by Khlebnikov (1885–1922) from *budet,* the future tense of "to be." Known today as "the father of Russian futurism," David Burlyuk (b. 1882) was one of the first echoes of French postimpressionism in art. Exuberant and indefatigable, this South Russian David roused, gathered, and tried to organize whatever individual rebels against the Goliath of convention he could discover. The Burlyuks (David was aided by his brothers, Vladimir and Nikolay) became a generic name for prewar iconoclasts. Equally facile with pen and brush, the brothers grouped together extremist painters, poets, composers, architects, stage directors, and other artists. Their exhibitions and public recitals furnished abundant food for sensation-mongering newspapers, whose conventional critics castigated the rebels unsparingly and unceremoniously as so much nameless riffraff. Before long a number of this riffraff became celebrities to be reckoned with, but at the moment the Burlyuks had hardly any respectable names on their list, beyond that of the versatile playwright and director, Nikolay Evreinov (b. 1879), and Dr. Nikolay Kulbin, Professor of the Military Medical Academy, State Councilor, and extremist painter, to whom reporters referred as "the mad doctor."

In 1909 the first collection of "budetlyane" poems was published by Burlyuk under the alliterate, and meaningless, title *Sadok sudey* ("Hatchery of Judges"). Illustrated by Vladimir Burlyuk and printed on the obverse side of cheap wallpaper, the booklet contained lyrics by Khlebnikov, David and Nikolay Burlyuk, Vasily Kamensky (b. 1884), Elena Guro, Myasoyedov, and Nizen. Marinetti's futurism was publicized one year later, and the cubo-futurist group was formed still later, their declaration, "A Slap in the Face of Public Taste," appearing, as we have seen, in 1912. So much for the chronology of inception: the few surviving cubo-futurists (Burlyuk, Kruchonykh, Kamensky) are jealous and touchy on this point. Be it as it may, the more consolidated activity of the group began after the publication of their declaration. Burlyuk organized a lecture tour through Russia, with Mayakovsky and Kamensky as fellow speakers and reciters. Burlyuk was responsible for turning Mayakovsky from painting (they had met as art students) to poetry. Kamensky, though still a student at the university, had already a reputation in literary circles (as subeditor of a review *Vesna*—"Spring"), and a much wider fame as a pioneer aviator, with some records and serious falls to his credit. The outlandishly groomed trio (Kamensky had an airplane painted on his forehead) spread the gospel of cubo-futurism through the country, drawing large crowds, and arousing curiosity mingled with indignation.

Both in his paintings and his poems Burlyuk illustrated his theory of art as a distortion of nature. In his speeches and essays he fought against all attempts at making art serve some outside purpose. As spokesman for his group, he objected not only to realism and its method of representation, but also to symbolism and its effort at transfiguration. Art must be above and beyond sense and ideas. "What you are saying," he wrote, "about contents, about spirituality, about ideas ... is the greatest crime against genuine art." The principle of "art for art's sake," under whatever guise, is always clearer in its negative than its positive implications. One finds it difficult to explain just what, outside of verbal innovations, the Burlyuk group sought to convey. Much later (in 1930), Burlyuk endeavored to formulate his theory under the term "entelechism," based on Aristotle's entelechy, but the new -ism has not helped matters. Burlyuk's early poetry was designed to shock the reader by new words and sounds, indifference to rules and manners, and a disregard for sense. Here is a specimen of his less extreme verse, as it appeared in an early collection, *Dokhlaya luna* ("Defunct Moon," 1914):

> Ev'rybody is young, is young, is young,
> In your belly hellish hunger,
> Well then, come, follow me . . .
> Behind my back
> A haughty call I throw,
> This short "speech":
> Let us eat rocks, grasses,
> Sweetness, bitters, poisons,
> Let us gobble emptiness,
> Depths and heights,
> Birds, beasts, monsters, fish,
> Wind, clay, salt and ripples!
> Ev'rybody is young, is young, is young,
> In your belly hellish hunger,
> Whatsoever we meet on the way
> May be used by us as food.

Since 1922, Burlyuk has lived in New York, where he occasionally exhibits his paintings and publishes his verse. Both his canvases and poems of this period have acquired "contents and ideas" which the earlier Burlyuk would have indicted as "the greatest crime against art." His poems, in particular, have been imbued with a social note, a protest against the misery and squalor which he observed in New York subways and parks, at the docks, and in kitchens for unemployed. Yet in the form of his verse Burlyuk remains unchanged, a living monument to the prewar *bu-*

detlyane. The introductory poem to his *Entelechial Verses* (1930)
is entitled in Newyorkese Russian: "Apseydaun [Upside-down]
Words," which might have been dated 1912:

> On trapezes of the mind for words to spin upside down,
> Generating mirrored walls, logic itself may command.
> Therein words will reflect, backside forward,
> And where hair used to be, a mouth may touchingly protrude.

Not all the members of the cubo-futurist group displayed the
cold, unemotional quality of Burlyuk. Elena Guro, for example,
one of the early *budetlyane* from the *Hatchery of Judges,* combined outlandish form with genuine emotion. Bereaved of her
little boy, Madame Guro became self-centered and well-nigh
monomaniacal in her grief for the lost baby. There is moving tenderness in her lines that make one visualize a stricken mother
crooning over an empty cradle. Even her neologisms are ingenuous
enough to lend her verse the air of a folk song. Such, for instance,
is the word *dolyanochka,* which she coined from *dolya,* fate:

> Fate, fate, little fate,
> Oh fate, quiet-quiet mine:
> What art thou to me? what am I to thee?
> But thou hast wearied me to death.

She could put pathos in such a common word as *nichevo,* meaning "it does not matter," " 'tis nothing," "it is all right":

> Now he laid himself down, calmed, dear—
> 'Tis nothing.
> Tender, funny, true, devoted—
> 'Tis nothing.
> Child of mine, dear baby,
> Clumsy, true child!
> Life itself I loved not
> So much as I loved you . . .
> In his wake life, too, goes—
> 'Tis nothing.
> There he is lying, so dear—
> 'Tis nothing.

Another contributor to the *Hatchery of Judges*, Vasily Kamensky, justly entitled his autobiography, published in 1931, *The Road of an Enthusiast*. Versatile and exuberant, he has "enthused" from his early childhood, and his geniality has endeared him to professionals of all sorts, from painters to aviators. Among his literary friends he counted realists, symbolists, futurists, feeling at home with Kuprin and Andreyev as much as with Blok, Severyanin, and the Burlyuks. His poetry is racy, melodious, and rather regular, despite certain verbal innovations and extremist declarations. His best-known poem before 1917, *Stepan Razin,* a daring description of the seventeenth-century rebel, appeared in defiance of war censorship. Typical of his lighter vein is

MY CAREER

Ever attuned for songs,
Ever a true friend to all,
I am all cloudlessly skyey,
I am a horizoned world-circle.

Poet, sage, and aviator,
Artist, lecturer, and *muzhik,*
I am all an elegant orator,
I am all the latest modish *chic.*

Like the carotid aorta rings
My narcotic lyricism—
From hamlet to sea-resort
I proclaim futurism.

Born in the Ural Mountains,
I was born a fierce eagle.
I know of no other morals
Than: Be free and forge ahead!

Despite their protestations of indifference to political or any other issues, some of the cubo-futurists exhaled a decided flavor of contempt for the *status quo,* which in those days inevitably implied sympathy for the revolutionary movement. Kamensky's

Stepan Razin, extolling the rebellious Cossacks of the seventeenth century, was easily interpreted as a call to action against the tsar. Mayakovsky was more direct in his onslaughts on the existing regime. Even Igor Severyanin, troubadour of boudoirs and champagne, when in the company of cubo-futurists, lisped mannered hatred. Thus, in their symposium *Moloko kobylits* ("Mares' Milk") Severyanin brandished a "fig for Peter" at the upper classes:

> In tuxedoes, hair parted *chic,* high-society dolts
> Tuned up in the Prince's parlor, sillified their faces.
> I smiled tensely, recalled gunpowder sarcasmly.
> A neopoetic motive sudden blew up boredom.
> Each line a blow in the face. My voice—solid mockery.
> Rhymes shape into insolent figs. Tongue sticks out assonance.
> I despise you flamingly, Your Lackluster Serenities,
> And to my despite I am counting on a world resonance!

Dismissing the slapstick verbiage of the futurists and the eccentricities of their verses and of their conduct, one must nevertheless take into account their efforts at revolutionizing both language and prosody. Along with their worthless tricks, they have given Russian poetry a more flexible vocabulary, as well as a greater freedom and variety of verse form.

This is exemplified in the much debated field of *zaúm* poetry. The futurists applied the word *zaúm* —"beyond sense," "irrational"—to the use of words, not for their meaning (they are often meaningless), but for the sake of invoking a certain picture or emotion. Thus, a rhythmic conglomeration of sounds might onomatopoetically suggest an Oriental city, or the Ukrainian speech. For illustration, Anton Lotov's "Melody of an Eastern City":

> Khan khan da dash   Vaks bar dan yak
> Shu shur i des   Zaza
> Vilar' yagda   Siu sech bazd i
> Suksan kaedeksh   Gar yo zda be
> Mak sa Mak sa   Men khatt zayde
> Yakim den zar   Vin da chok me.

Similarly meaningless are the words of Vasilisk Gnedov, but they are close enough to actual Ukrainian sounds to create the illusion of genuine Ukrainian:

Hriba budik tsiri chipich—
Zdvina na kham dyaki,
Koli za hich budin tsikavche
Taras Sherchenko budyache skavche—
Hulya laskav stohma rehota tsvirka
Svitina zzila sankeh.
Baydry shliha shkapik ruko
Da d'hoti sila khmara
A ya z zirok poiv oparu.

Some of the extremists reached the limits of absurdity in their efforts to set the word free from meaning. Alexander Kruchonykh (b. 1886) and his faction preached the enthronement of sound not merely at the expense of, but to the exclusion of, sense. At first they directed their *zaúm* attempts to the coinage of new words for old concepts. Kruchonykh assigned this task to the poet, for whom he claimed the right to see the world in a novel way, as Adam did, and like him to give new names to things. "The lily is beautiful," he wrote earlier in his career, "but the word 'lily' is atrocious; it has been handled a good deal, and raped. Therefore I name the lily 'yeouyi'—the pristine beauty is restored." This dubious improvement of human speech failed, however, to satisfy Kruchonykh any more than such reforms as the abolition of punctuation marks and rules of orthography, of meter and rhyme, or the "shattering" of grammar and syntax. He later declared war against meaning in poetry. Lermontov's melodious lyric, "The Angel," he branded as food "apt to upset the stomach of a robust person," and against sucn poetry he set forth as superior fare his own concoction of meaningless sounds:

dir, bull, schchill,   vi so boo
oubeshchour   r l ehz
skoom

Parenthetically he commented: "In these five lines there is more of the national Russian spirit than in all the poetry of Pushkin." One could hardly go beyond Kruchonykh. Indeed, his brand of futurism ended in a *cul de sac,* in a Gertrude Steinesque incoherence that lacked even a saving grace of musical suggestiveness.

Far superior was the acknowledged leader of the *zaúm* poetry, Victor (renamed by himself "Velemir") Khlebnikov. He had an intimate knowledge of the Russian language, an inborn feeling for words and their architectonics, and a natural penchant for philological adventures. These qualities he betrayed in his most daring innovations and nonsense verses, thus differing from most of the futurists, who depended on whim and intuition when taking liberties with grammar and speech. Khlebnikov won his initial fame by a poem in which the word *smyekh,* laughter, was used in an endless variety of derivatives, most of them fantastic, but all marked with an authentic sound true to the flexibility of Russian prefixes and suffixes.

The dancing hilarity of Khlebnikov's poem defies transmission into another tongue. I have nevertheless attempted an approximate version, keeping the original meter and rhythm:

> Oh, laugh forth, laugh laughadors!
> Oh, laugh on, laugh laughadors!
> You who laugh in laughs, laugh-laugh, you who laughorize so laughly,
>   Laugh forth, laugh laugh belaughly!
> Oh, of laughdom overlaughy, laugh of laughish laughadors!
> Oh, forth laugh downright laughly, laugh of super-laughadors!
>   Laughery! Laughery!
> Belaugh, uplaugh, laughikins, laughikins,
>   Laughutelets, laughutelets!
> Oh, laugh forth, laugh laughadors!
> Oh, laugh on, laugh laughadors![7]

---

[7] And here is the original:
    O, rassmeytyes', smyekhachi!
    O, zasmeytyes', smyekhachi!
Chto smyeyutsa smyekhami, chto smyeyanstvuyut smyeyalno,

Along with his genuine contributions to linguistic poetics, and his numerous graceful if nonsensical verses, Khlebnikov wrote on occasion with pompous gravity, signing his "Command": "King of Time, Velemir." There is a mixture of the messianic and the megalomaniac in the futurist proclamation "Marsian Trumpet," where one discerns Khlebnikov behind such lines as these:

We who are clad in the cloak of sheer victories are about to build a young guild, with its sails around the axis of time, giving warning beforehand that our dimensions are greater than those of Cheops, and our task is audacious, majestic, serene. . . . We are beautiful in our unflinching treason to the past, the moment it has reached the age of victory, and in the steadfast fury of the swing of our sledgehammer across the globe which is already trembling from the stamp of our feet. Black sails of Time, boom!

The one futurist who stood out from the very beginning, and who at no moment remained static, was Vladimir Mayakovsky. His name appeared among the signers of "A Slap in the Face of Public Taste," and of subsequent declarations of the cubo-futurists. But declarations and theories are one thing, and creative literature quite another. This has been evidenced in many authentic poets, particularly Mayakovsky. What distinguished him from most of his fellow futurists was the element of robust sense which he displayed even in his extreme innovations and outlandish stunts. His work will be discussed presently, when I deal with literature after 1917: Mayakovsky's poetry naturally overlaps both periods and splashes over and across the revolutionary years. At this point it should be noted that even before 1917, when he sounded blatantly far-fetched and insolent, and flaunted his notorious yellow shirt-

---

O, zasmeytyes' usmyeyalno!
O, rassmyeshishch nadsmeyalnykh smyekh usmeynykh smyekhachey!
O, issmeysa rassmeyalno smyekh nadsmeynykh smeyachey!
Smeyevo! Smeyevo!
Usmey, osmey, smyeshiki, smyeshiki
Smeyunchiki, smeyunchiki!
O, rassmeytyes', smekhachi!
O, zasmeytyes', smyekhachi!

waist (retrospectively: " 'Tis good to hide your soul from inspection by wrapping it in a yellow waist"), he showed on occasion keen judgment and a perspicacity that was almost prophetic. Such was his paper "A Drop of Tar" (the Russian saying, "A spoon of tar in a barrel of honey," is akin to the English, "A fly in the ointment"), published in December, 1915, as an imaginary funeral oration on the reputed death of futurism. Here he foreshadows the change of futurism from the precious shriek of a handful of solipsists into the clarion call of a great revolution. You feel in this "dirge" both the spirit of the war that was raging at the moment and the portent of the oncoming national upheaval. He chides the traditional critics and the middle-aged readers ("the young men, to whom we are endeared, will not be back from the battlefield for some time yet") for jeering at the corpse: "Gentlemen, aren't you really sorry for this giddy red-tufted chap who admittedly was not so clever, and a bit boorish, but always, oh, always daring and ardent?" He admits, though, that he himself is not so sorry for the deceased, "for different reasons, to be sure." He asks them to recall the "first gala appearance of Russian futurism, signalized by that ringing 'slap in the face of public taste,' " with its three memorable blows: against all canons that "reduce inspiration to ice," against the old language, "too feeble to catch up with life's gallop," and finally against "the old great," the Pushkins, Dostoyevskys, Tolstoys, to be "thrown overboard from the steamship of modernity." This declaration of destructiveness and anarchism, derided by the philistines as the "eccentricity of madmen," "has proved to be a diabolical intuition embodied in the stormy Today," owing to the all-broadening effect of the war. The war and the impending "unknown" prompt Mayakovsky to call for new dimensions and new approaches: "Painter! Will you attempt to capture speeding cavalry with the tiny net of contours? . . . Poet! Do not seat a mighty battle in the rocking chair of iambics and trochees. . . . Who can discern behind a Cossack whoop the warble of mandolinist Bryusov?"

The new voice, born of war and of the revolution already glimmering on the horizon, Mayakovsky defines as futurism:

> Today we are all futurists! The nation is futurist!
> *Futurism has clutched Russia in an inescapable grip.*
> Failing to see futurism ahead of you, and incapable of peering into your-
> selves, you have raised the cry about its death. Yes, futurism is dead—as
> a particular group, but it has suffused you all as a flood. Well, since futur-
> ism as an idea of the chosen few is dead, we no longer need it. The first,
> the destructive part of our program, we regard as completed. Don't be
> surprised, then, if today you observe in our hands the design of an archi-
> tect in place of the jester's rattle, and if the voice of futurism, yesterday
> still soft from sentimental dreaminess, shall pour forth with the vigor of
> a sermon.

This was written in 1915! What sounded then like the raving of
a maniac turned out to be the keen anticipation of a seer.

Chapter III ✦ 1917 and After

THE MOVEMENTS briefly surveyed in the preceding pages had one trait in common: they all reflected the moribund order from which they sprang. The note of decadence rang, now muted, now shrill, in the verses of the early symbolists and of their offshoots, from the acmeists to the futurists. These poets strove to escape from the immediate and the actual, and above all from "the street." Self-centered and obscure, they appealed to a limited audience, an élite capable of enjoying the unusual, the esoteric, the distorted and unhealthy, and thereby demonstrating its superiority to ordinary humanity. Like the Western world, Russia on the eve of the war of 1914–1918 showed signs of satiety and indigestion within its social organism, which needed such drastic purgatives as war and revolution. One of these universal symptoms might be seen in the efflorescence of nonrealistic art, of postimpressionism, futurism, cubism, expressionism, dadaism, and other ostrich-like attempts to bury one's head against seeing the doomed state of affairs. Art has a subtle way of recording social conditions by way of style and form.

In Russia, more than elsewhere, the war proved an "acid test" for the moral and material preparedness of the country. Having failed utterly in the test, tsarist Russia gave up the ghost, to the nearly unanimous joy of the nation and the satisfaction of the Allies, who now expected a more vigorous prosecution of the war. Within a few months, however, it became evident that the revolution was not only political but also social. Uncivilized, that is, untrained in the flexible methods of compromise, the Russian masses once aroused demanded all or nothing. The only leadership that augured success had to display a sense of realism and an ability to gauge the psychological moment. Such was the leadership of Lenin and his faction, who offered the people the very things they had clamored for—peace, land, and bread. The victorious Bolsheviks began at once negotiations for an armistice with the Central Powers, the land was declared nationalized, and as to bread, which was used as an inclusive term—all available resources, including mines, factories, banks, and public utilities, became the property of the people, who were henceforth to share the country's opulence and poverty alike.

The far-reaching thoroughness of the Bolshevik Revolution startled the intelligentsia. The new measures were so drastic, unheard of, as to seem a nightmare to those who through them were deprived of their privileges and often of their subsistence even. A nightmare does not last long, was the consoling thought. "Two weeks," became the whispered password; two weeks was the longest the bolshevik bad dream was expected to last, what with the bristling hostility of the whole civilized world, and the opposition of the "better" classes within the nation. Lenin (1870–1924) himself was not sure that the experiment would outlast the span of the French Commune of 1871. This attitude accounts for the widespread boycott or strike against the bolshevik "usurpers" on the part of the intelligentsia, whether they were bank officers or foreign-ministry experts, engineers or switchboard operators, painters or authors, and whether they were reactionary monarchists or liberals, moderate socialists or political indifferentists. When, in November, 1917, the new government called for a conference of authors and artists at Petrograd, there came five men in all: the poets Blok, Mayakovsky, Ivnev (b. 1893), the painter N. Altman (b. 1889), and one representative of the theater, Vsevolod Meierhold (b. 1874).

Only two well-known writers had the temerity to join the Bolshevik regime from the outset, V. Bryusov and A. Serafimovich. Both were denounced and ostracized as traitors who had sold themselves. When the "two weeks" had become an elastic symbol, and hunger compelled the intelligentsia to seek some employment or other from the authorities, their hostility to the regime lost, not its intensity, but its blatancy. Such periodicals as appeared from time to time during those lean years voiced gloom, despondency, and apocalyptic forebodings. This was true even of such publications as *The Home of Arts,* or *Notes of Dreamers,* whose contributors were not outspoken enemies of the new order. Among the "dreamers" were A. Bely, A. Blok, V. Ivanov, and other prominent symbolists, who "accepted" the revolution but found it impossible to transform themselves overnight and to adjust their lifelong individualistic notions to the collectivist outlook; hence their nostalgic reveries. More definitely pessimistic were the irreconcilable "inner emigrants," the peevish "lovers of the people" who now found themselves unappreciated and even brushed aside by the forward-marching people. They had anticipated the revolution, even glorified its advent when it seemed so remote and abstract. The realized revolution proved harsh, rude, and not so romantic. Y. Aikhenvald (1872–1928), a literary critic of note, found "a certain inner contradiction in the conception of a 'victorious revolutionist,' since the revolutionist ceases to be one as soon as he is victorious." This was a frank formulation of what numerous ladies and gentlemen, erstwhile sympathizers with the revolution, felt upon its triumph. Another "lover of the people," A. Petrishchev, discovered the ingratitude of the people toward their champions and leaders, their superiors who always organize and prepare revolutions, and are discarded the morning after, when "Sancho Panza ... demands that Don Quixote now be his armor bearer. Since this demand cannot possibly be fulfilled, Don Quixote is declared a traitor and is executed." Changing similes, Petrishchev compares the role of the intelligentsia to that of Columbus, whose services are employed to discover America, but who is thrown into prison and is replaced by the conquistadors when America is to be exploited. Typical of this mood of disenchantment is a leading editorial in the review *Messenger of Literature,* late in the year

1921, when passions had had time to cool off. A few characteristic passages follow:

Heavy are the trials which contemporary reality imposes upon us, representatives of the much-suffering Russian intelligentsia. First of all, material privations have come down on our heads. Even formerly we barely made ends meet, yet we were far from feeling like beggars. Now we face actual penury, for our mental labor yields us earnings many times smaller than the pittance that used to be received not only by doormen and janitors but even by day laborers. So as not to die from hunger we sell and trade our last belongings. Most of us have neither adequate boots nor decent clothes.... And how many of us have perished in recent years!

But from hunger and cold only the body suffers. The tragedy of our situation consists in that, however great the physical sufferings we have experienced, they are completely overshadowed by our spiritual sufferings. These date from the beginning of the new era of Russian life, the era created by the February revolution of 1917. With what ecstasy the intelligentsia greeted the revolution, how ardently they believed that it would put an end to their separation from the people. How bitterly they proved mistaken, how soon they became convinced that their hopes met with no sympathetic echo among the people, that the people placed the intelligentsia in the same brackets with the "exploiters," the "bourgeois," the "gentry," and therefore regarded them with unconcealed animosity.

Three years of civil strife, and the display of selfishness and all varieties of commercial "speculation" that went with it, have forced the intelligentsia to change their opinion about the people. Disappointment in the people has become general, and in the wake of this disappointment in the people had to come, and come it did, disappointment in ourselves. If we were so cruelly mistaken in our opinion of the people, if the postrevolutionary reality has to such a degree deceived our expectations, then we ourselves are of no use whatever, so far as we claim the role of "builders of a new edifice," seekers of new roads. Disappointment in ourselves has acquired an ever-growing effect over our minds, because we have seen more and more often how the turgid current of selfishness and cupidity has been engulfing many of us into its foul bosom.... For those it has carried off, there is no salvation.... Nothing can atone for the sin of a mentally and morally developed man who has deliberately joined those who "crucify their Christ, who sell their fatherland." However, though the number of those who have yielded to temptation is great, still greater is the number of those who have resisted the temptation. But to overcome the lure of self-interest does not yet mean to cease being disappointed in oneself and in the people. The burden of this double disappointment is equivalent to the bearing of death in one's soul. No creative work toward building new forms of life is thinkable without faith in the people and faith in oneself. There remains only one thing to do: with drooping arms to resign oneself and one's native land to the will of circumstances.

This somewhat lengthy quotation embodies the traits of most of the intelligentsia, their trite phraseology, mistiness, sentimentality, conceited humility and self-righteousness, and utter impotence. To be sure, from the end of the eighteenth century on, an effective handful of members of the intelligentsia displayed nobility, heroism, and self-sacrifice which have served as a challenging legacy to their countrymen. The quoted lines, however, voiced the epigoni of the intelligentsia, the Bryonic Hamlets of Russian life, who, in the style of Turgenev, "folded impotent arms on an empty breast," and tried to remain in this tragicomic pose, while history was rushing by. No wonder the revolution swept these whimpering Chekhovian Ivanovs into the "dustbin of history," and brought about their gradual replacement by a new intelligentsia, strong of will, replete with energy, and capable of action.

The poets fared better than the prose writers: in any event their voices were not silenced. With the few exceptions noted before, they continued to write, and, when this was feasible, to publish. Even those young poets who eventually migrated abroad and passed over to the enemy side, like Tsvetayeva (b. 1892), Khodasevich (1886–1939), Adamovich (b. 1894), and others, contributed verse to sporadic Soviet reviews and miscellanies that were wretchedly printed on sleazy paper. The symbolists showed marked vigor in those days of bewilderment and intellectual apathy. Owing to their erudition and polyglot qualifications, leading symbolists were in demand as lecturers, translators and editors of foreign classic and modern works, under the enlightenment policies of Commissar Lunacharsky (1875–1933) and the unofficial guardian of Russia's cultural values, Maxim Gorky. The promptly bolshevized Valery Bryusov was not the only symbolist entrusted with important and responsible duties in the field of literary, particularly poetic, education. "Neutral" poets, as for example Andrey Bely and Alexander Blok, were also kept extremely busy trying to satisfy the suddenly aroused thirst for knowledge on the part of the masses. Among other things. Bely conducted poetry classes among workers. Blok had his hands full with reading papers and reciting his poetry for large audiences, and editing literary and historical publications.

So far as creative poetry was concerned, the masterpiece of that early period was, of course, Blok's *The Twelve*. Extremely sensitive, well-nigh clairvoyant, Blok has succeeded in what is rarely attained by art, namely, in giving expression to contemporary turbulence, without the benefit of perspective in time or space. Neither music nor literature, let alone the other arts, has as yet reflected the initial phase of the Bolshevik Revolution with the quintessential succinctness of *The Twelve*. The poem is a symphony of the October upheaval, as complex and as simple, as brutally direct and as surcharged with portents. Through the variety of its motives and rhythms runs the dominant note of a *chastushka*—a rustic folk jingle. Twelve Red Guardsmen march through the streets of Petrograd in a howling blizzard. They swear and blaspheme, they fire and kill, they threaten to destroy Holy Russia and its cowed capital. This poem of blood, misery, heartache, and the pathos of groping forward, is brought to an unexpected end, to the refrain of

Trakh-takh-takh!   By bullet unharmed,
Trakh-takh-takh!   Softly treading above the blizzard,
Thus they march with lordly step.   In a halo of snowy diamonds,
Behind—a hungry mongrel,   And a wreath of roses white,
Ahead—with a bloody banner,   Ahead—marches Jesus Christ.[1]
Unseen behind the snowstorm,

[1] Religious and antireligious notes lingered on in Russian literature for some time after 1917. Blok's reference to Christ, in *The Twelve*, was echoed in Bely's lyrics on

The Twelve was hailed by the Bolsheviks and by their enemies alike; both "causes" claimed the poem. Most likely, Blok himself was not entirely aware of its definite partisanship. His best poetry was not of cognitive source, but purely inspirational, resulting from that "mystic ecstasy" of which he speaks in his self-revelatory poem *The Artist. The Twelve* showed Blok's unrivaled and uncanny ability to "listen to the revolution." The very acceptance of the poem by antagonistic groups testifies to its catholic appeal as a national masterpiece. With this one glorious exception, the revolution has not been adequately recorded as yet in a work of art. Blok himself wrote only one other poem of note about the same time as he composed *The Twelve,* namely *Scythians,* in which he addressed the Western nations on behalf of Russia, land of the Eurasian Scythians. There is fire and force in the poem, but by the side of *The Twelve* it is like a trombone solo compared with an orchestrated symphony. Blok, like Bely, Bryusov, and other symbolists, and for that matter like most of the established writers, including Gorky, found the moment too tumultuous for creative imaginary work. The moment, furthermore, laid stress on utilitarian values, and men of education were called upon to expend their time and energy in responding to the elemental cry for enlightenment. Consider, in addition, that the closer the artist had been bound up with the life and moods of Yesterday, the more difficult it was for him to readjust himself so as to fit in with the Morning After.

Russia ("Christ Has Risen," e.g.), and in a number of verses by such peasant-poets as Klyuyev, Klychkov, and Oreshin. Yesenin often used images and similes suffused with a religious hue, but at times they border on the sacrilegious. Openly antireligious motifs began to appear in the poems of Yesenin's fellow imagist, Mariengof. His crude, almost obscene allusions to Christ and the other members of the Trinity served as a keynote for antireligious writings and cartoons during the heyday of militant atheism. By the 1930's, however, both religious and sacrilegious references were seldom used by Soviet authors. The public mind was growing irreligious, but less antireligious. Symptomatic of this change has been the increasingly tolerant policy of the government toward the church. The authorities rebuked such attempts at ridiculing the old church as that of Demyan Bedny in his comedy, *The Ancient Heroes* (see p. 147 below).

Chapter IV ✦ Postsymbolists

FUTURISTS (CONTINUED)

THE DIFFICULTY for men with deep-rooted traditions to adjust themselves to a new order may explain, in part and inversely, the vogue of the futurists during that period. Their bonds with the past were quite tenuous, and for them it presented no hardship to go over unreservedly to the new order. On the other hand, the Bolshevik authorities, isolated and ostracized from within and without, could ill afford to reject the only group of artists who offered their support. There is an old Russian saying: "Where fish are scarce, even a crayfish is a fish." While most of the known artists opposed the new rule, or hesitated, or accepted it halfheartedly, the futurists came out for it promptly and unequivocally. Lunacharsky and other spokesmen for the proletariat did not relish these erstwhile bad boys of literature, these eccentric verbal brawlers and scandalizers of the public taste, these typical voices of a decaying and moribund civilization; but this was hardly the time for fastidiousness: can beggars be choosers? Thus it came about that the first workers' government gave its sanction and support to an extreme art current that was remote from the understanding and appreciation of the just-awakened masses. Futurists of all variants and shades, painters, sculptors, architects, stage directors, poets, predominated in the official life of Russia for some time after the Bolshevik victory. "In the backwoods even Tom passes for a nobleman," to quote another Russian proverb.

Social-revolutionary futurism sounds like a paradox, yet it is dialectically plausible for the offspring of a social order to turn against its begetter. In the destructive part of their program Russian futurists followed their parent, Marinetti, and his Italo-French group of enemies of traditions and museums, of grammar and authority. But whereas Marinetti's worship of speed and the machine brought him and his adherents into the arms of militarism, imperialism, and fascism, their Russian counterpart embraced the Soviet regime from its very outset. Ridiculed and despised by the society which they represented, entertained, and hated at the same time, the Russian futurists greeted the Bolshevik Revolution as a complete divorce from the past. Hatred of conventions and the past may be purely negative and destructive, unless it be coupled with a positive, constructive element. Practical bolshevism was to go through this test, as well as the theories and tendencies it sponsored. In the early part of its rule bolshevism was engaged primarily in destroying inimical ideas and institutions, in clearing the ground for new construction. Aside, then, from the "crayfish" reasoning, the futurists were welcomed because their destructive attack against Yesterday fell in line with the official policy of the moment.

This odd marriage, in large measure one of convenience, did not last long. The rank and file of the proletariat, and also most of its leaders, could not stomach the futurist fare, and, though suffering it as one of the extraordinary features of war and revolution, they frowned upon the extravagances of their outlandish friends. Constructivist scenery and designs for buildings and monuments, suprematist ("abstract expressionist") painting and sculpture, bloodthirsty but incoherent verse, fantastic pageants, in which impossible colors distorted the naturalness of grass and trees— these and similar "abstractions" failed to register in the proletarian mind. The organ of proletarian writers, *Gryadushcheye* ("Days to Come") protested against the spread of futurist art. In its issue for December, 1918, P. Bessalko (1880–1920), one of the first authors from the workers' ranks, voiced the opinion of the more moderate "creators of proletarian art," in allowing that "one might utilize a few valuable things out of their [the futurists'] technical baggage," but he too insisted that "in no case should they be permitted to clothe the body of workers' culture in futuristic garments." The proletarian note in Soviet letters, and the battles waged over it, will be discussed presently. At this point it should be noted that, in spite of the natural and popular resentment against them, the futurists, by their professed loyalty, won the toleration and even the support of the government that was chafing under isolation at home and abroad. Thus, they were given charge of *The Art of the Commune,* organ of the art section of the Commissariat of People's Education.

In this official publication the recently despised outcasts assumed an authoritative, if not totalitarian, tone. Representatives of the graphic arts were especially vociferous: they virtually demanded the dictatorship of a handful of hitherto unrecognized artists over all art. "Only futurist art is at the present moment the art of the proletariat," declared N. Altman. A complete discarding of the past was the leading motive. According to N. Punin, "To blow up, demolish, wipe off the face of the earth the old forms of art— such must be the dream of the new artist, the proletarian artist, the new man." This artist has to go down to factories, mines, foundries, to saturate himself with the actualities of the working masses, and to create new things in a new manner. V. Mayakovsky, the spokesman of literature in this group, was in full accord with his fellow contributors. In a public symposium arranged by the official Art Section on the subject, "Temple or Factory," Mayakovsky said, among other things:

What we need is not a dead temple of art, wherein languish dead productions, but a living workshop of the human mind. We want a hardy-rye art, rye words, rye deeds. Our present-day art is not good for anything. The old subjects and landscapes speak only the gossip of the rich and the bourgeois. It is a pity that artists waste their talents on such needless things. Art must be focused not in dead temple-museums, but everywhere: in streets, in tramcars, in factories, in workshops, and in workers' quarters.

At that time Mayakovsky also regarded futurism as the only adequate expression of proletarian art, asserting that old forms are

incapable of mirroring the new life. He questioned the good faith
of the nonfuturist intelligentsia who began to flock to the Soviet
order when the "two weeks" slogan had dwindled into an unful-
filled wish. At a public discussion of "The Proletariat and Art,"
held in Petrograd in December, 1918, Mayakovsky took exception
to the conciliatory remarks of the main speaker, who greeted all
those willing to come into the fold and help create a proletarian art.

> You say [he shouted]: "Welcome to our midst." We say: "Show your
> credentials." Which is it that has sent you here—a heart beating in time
> with the proletarian revolution, or a thirst for orders from the new master?
> All those who yesterday debated whether they ought to shake hands with
> us, have now readily adapted the new ideas; we shall not be fooled by that.
> The new must be spoken of with new words. A new form of art is wanted.
> It is not enough to erect a monument to the metal worker: one must see
> to it that it differs from the monument raised by the tsar to the printer.
> The revolution, which has divided Russia into two camps, has drawn a
> boundary also between right and left art. To the left are we, inventors of
> the new; to the right are they, those who regard art as a means for sundry
> acquisitions [a play on words: the same word, *obretat'*, means, when pre-
> fixed by *iz*, "to invent," and with the prefix *pri-*, "to acquire"]. The work-
> ers have understood this splendidly, and they have met our appearances
> with joy. There is no classless art. The proletariat alone, and only in our
> land, will create new art.

That the masses "met their appearances with joy" was true
mainly with regard to Mayakovsky. The sturdy poet, towering
above his audience and declaiming in a thundering bass his unique
yet clear and incisive verses or speeches, appealed to revolutionary
Russia. It was also known that a group of Petrograd workers had
attempted to organize as a Comfut Collective (the Party refused
to register them as a branch of communist-futurists). On the whole,
however, the working masses and their leaders, while enjoying
some of the futurist poetry, particularly when delivered by such a
tribune as Mayakovsky, had no use for the "doctrine" of futurism.
As a matter of fact, even the poetry failed to please the palates of

orthodox Bolsheviks; Lenin would be overcome by sleep after reading a few lines by Mayakovsky. Even the broadminded and lenient Lunacharsky was constrained to take issue with the futurists and their bombastic claims. Two of their tenets were especially resented by the Bolsheviks: the sweeping rejection of the past, and the pretension to an exclusive leadership and control of proletarian art. As we shall see later, the authorities had to combat similar monopolistic notions by the extreme opposites of the futurists, from the early Proletcult groups to the RAPP. Lunacharsky tried to tame the overzealous "revolutionaries" (incidentally, his lenience was repeatedly censured by the Central Committee of the Party), chiding them but at the same time not withdrawing his official support. A mild polemic took place in the pages of *The Art of the Commune* between the Commissar of Education and the champions of a totalitarian futurism. Lunacharsky was finally provoked by the pontifical tone of this organ, supposed to be the voice of his department. After the publication of a zealot poem by Mayakovsky, " 'Tis Too Early to Rejoice," Lunacharsky sent in a letter to the editors, from which I quote a few lines:

> Two traits in your young periodical frighten me somewhat: its destructive tendencies toward the past, and its attempt while speaking in the name of a definite school to speak at the same time in the name of the government.
>
> Surely not in vain have we exerted so many, at times heroic, efforts for the preservation of every variety of old art ..., and we cannot permit an official organ of our Commissariat to present our whole art legacy, from Adam to Mayakovsky, as a heap of rubbish subject to destruction.
>
> On the other hand ...
>
> There is nothing wrong about the fact that the government of workers and peasants has given considerable support to artist-innovators: these had been cruelly cast out by the older men. Not only were the futurists the first to come to the aid of the revolution; not only have they proved, of all the intelligentsia, the most congenial and responsive to the revolution; they have actually shown themselves fine organizers in many fields. ...

But it would be wrong if the artist-innovators presumed to regard themselves as a *state* school working for an official, albeit revolutionary, art dictated from above.[1]

This abnormal situation could not last long, and no one illustrated its abnormality more clearly than Mayakovsky himself. Mayakovsky must be treated separately, as *the* poet of the revolution, which stimulated his growth and absorbed fully his strength, talent, and time. After 1917 he personified whatever was vital and creative in futurism, and his desperate efforts at harnessing his Pegasus to the chariot of a proletarian revolution proved pathetic. From 1923 to 1930, the year of his death, Mayakovsky made at least four public shifts of his position in the direction of proletarian orthodoxy. These shifts showed the catastrophic maladjustment of Mayakovsky, whose suicide brought an end to the chapter of futurism in its various ramifications.

As a movement, futurism collapsed in the early nineteen twenties, both because of its tactless claims and its sterility. With all their vociferous pretensions, the futurists' net contributions to the

---

[1] Mayakovsky's poem, not reprinted in his collected works, read in part:

A White Guardist
You uncover—and up with him against
  the wall.
But Raphael have you forgotten?
Have you forgotten Rastrelli?*
'Tis time
with bullets
to tattoo museum walls.
Shoot at the old rubbish from hundred-
  inch maws!
You are sowing death in the enemy
  camp.

Doomed are capital's hirelings.
Yet Tsar Alexander
in the Square of Insurrections
is standing.
Thither your dynamite!
Arrayed are your cannon near
  the woods,
Impervious to White Guards'
  amenities.
But why isn't Pushkin attacked?
And other
classic generals?

* An eighteenth-century architect who designed several palaces and monuments for official Russia.

The *Art of the Commune* "explained," in the course of the polemic, that Mayakovsky did not mean to be literal. The poet himself resented, in a subsequent public discussion, the accusation "of instigating violence against old art." He himself was "ready to place chrysanthemums on Pushkin's grave. But should the dead emerge from their graves and pretend to influence the art of our day, they must be told that there can be no place for them among the living. . . . The leading role in art must remain with the new men."

art life of the new state were puny. What they actually produced, as a group, was laughably incommensurate with their solemn declarations and manifestoes. Individual futurists, in poetry and in other arts, proceeded to create and develop, with or without the benefit of -ism labels. But as a literary current, futurism had outlived itself in the early 'twenties, after having served its role of a shakeup and a stimulant. The effect of futurism on Russian poetry is felt to this day. Its cleansing campaign against hackneyed forms, words, and images influenced not only such of its variants as imagism or constructivism, but, paradoxically enough, even the best of the purely proletarian poets.

Mayakovsky.—Vladimir Mayakovsky (1893–1930) deserves special notice because he was *the* poet of revolutionary Russia, in the same way as Vladimir Lenin was its organizer and leader. He personified and expressed the new order—a husky seven-footer striding the length and breadth of the earth, his thundering bass roaring staccatoes unheard of in form and of shocking contents. In lyric and epic, in satire and epigram, in drama on stage and screen, in poster and placard and marching song, in print and from the platform, Mayakovsky gave voice to the issues and events of Soviet Russia's formative years. About nine-tenths of his voluminous output reflects phases of Russian reality after November, 1917, from the uprising itself through the civil wars, intervention, and blockade, the "breathing spell" interlude of the NEP (New Economic Policy), and into the constructive era of the first Five-Year Plan. Mayakovsky's pen and bass performed a double service: on the one hand, they glorified the achievements of the revolution, they sang the courage of the masses, the Red soldiers and sailors, the Young Communists, the might of the collective "Ivan," the greatness and simplicity of Lenin. At the same time, Mayakovsky brandished his weapons to condemn and satirize the enemies of the revolution, the external as well as the lurking inner enemies— stupidity, ignorance, selfishness, pettiness, vulgarity, bureaucratic red tape, and other survivals of the old philistia. While his work suffers occasionally from unevenness, raucous exaggeration, slipshod wording and structure—in a word, journalistic carelessness—it attains on the whole the goal of lending to the revolution a distinct style. In popularity he may have been eclipsed by so clear and colloquial a poet as Demyan Bedny (b. 1883), but Demyan Bedny's verse, aside from its subject matter, might belong to any prerevolutionary period since the days of Ivan Krylov (1768–1844). Mayakovsky's main contribution was precisely a style of the revolution. He had the satisfaction of feeling that this contribution would not end with his early death, for even in his lifetime his style found able followers and continuers. In Aseyev, Selvinsky, Bezymensky, and others, the Mayakovsky chord vibrates, with variations, to this day.

The 1915 prophecy of Mayakovsky, previously mentioned, appeared to him fulfilled in October, 1917. The Bolshevik Revolution, with its sweeping abolition of institutions, beliefs, traditions, attitudes, and relationships, appealed to him as a cleansing hurricane, and won him over at once and fully. He was the only prominent poet, next to Bryusov, to have placed himself unreservedly at the service of the new order immediately upon its introduction. The last thirteen years of his life, his most active years, were wholly dedicated to the gigantic tasks that confronted the country. He did not hesitate to use his pen for "propaganda"; in fact, nearly everything he wrote during that time was propaganda in behalf of the newly found ideal. In his teens, as an impecunious art student in Moscow (he was born and reared in the Caucasus), he had joined the Bolshevik faction of the Social Democratic Party, and was active enough to merit eleven months in prison. His allegiance was, however, skin-deep, and upon his release he entered the ranks of the Moscow bohemia, living boisterously and without aim, hating his environment, and harboring only destructive passions. The October revolution filled him with a purpose, gave vent to his hatred, and imbued him with a positive aspiration—to build a new life over the ruins of the old. How could he help being a champion, a propagandist of the ideal that absorbed his entire being and dictated his thoughts and feelings and actions? He put all of himself into his work, whether it was a long epic, a play, or a poster, a caricature (he drew powerful cartoons), a militant slogan, a short and poignant satire on one of the many evils and issues of the day. Whatever came from his pen had the sparkle of his talent, the unmistakable Mayakovsky touch that distinguished every utterance of his, regardless of the subject matter. Form was to him all-important: the form in which the revolution could be expressed was to be as fresh and new as the very contents of the new life. Thus futurism was not an external whim with Mayakovsky, but an inseparable essence of his creative self—and of the revolution.

Mayakovsky's theoretical views were neither solid nor immutable; in any event, their effect on his poetry was rather uncertain. His confidence in the wisdom of the Communist Party impelled him to modify these views time and again, with no apparent detriment to the quality of his productions. In 1923, he organized the LEF (Left Front) group, its organ advocating a policy which seemed to be a departure from pure futurism, though its slogan, factualism, presented another variety of the formalistic heresy.[2] Four years later he began to publish *The New LEF,* more proletarian in tone, but in September, 1928, he withdrew from the group, and delivered a public address, "To the Left of LEF." One year later he organized the group REF (Revolutionary Front), and in February, 1930, two months before his death, he joined the RAPP (Russian Association of Proletarian Writers), at the moment considered one hundred per cent orthodox and loyal. This shift of groups and labels need not be taken seriously so far as Mayakovsky's poetic integrity is concerned, but it is evident that the question where he should "belong" did trouble his mind, and might

---

[2] For the formalistic controversy see pages 89–97, below.

have contributed to the final catastrophe—of which presently. Whatever his theoretic vagaries, they did not prevent him from serving the new order in a tirelessly dynamic fashion, with pen and brush and voice, ever on the go, addressing public meetings, soldiers, factory workers in every part of vast Russia and even abroad, through Europe and the Americas.

Buffon's maxim is most strikingly illustrated by Mayakovsky, for style and man were in him nearly one and the same. Elemental by nature and scantily educated, Mayakovsky grew up as a "grand primitive," regarding himself and life with wonderment and admiration, and unburdened by traditions and all superimposed rules and forms. He was enraptured with his self, the man in him, with his two fine arms that "can move from the right to the left and from the left to the right," with his "precious mind," sparkling in the jewel box of a cranium, with his marvelous red tongue, a voice that can shout "oh-ho-ho," and that "extraordinary lump beating under the wool of his waistcoat" (*Man*, 1916). This primitive resents society, the tyrant that clips man's wings, chains him, and emasculates life. In his satirical "Hymn to the Judge" (1915), galley slaves sing of their Peruvian paradise destroyed by a judge with eyes—"a pair of tin cans glimmering in a garbage hole." The judge's eye, "austere like Lent," causes the magnificent tail of an orange-blue peacock to "fade momentarily." As for the colibri that flew in the prairies, the judge has captured them and shaved their "down and feathers." He has shut down the flaming volcanoes that rose from the valleys, putting up signs: "This Valley for Nonsmokers." Of course, he has put a ban on Mayakovsky's verses, as "another intoxicating drink." Man-made tyranny in all its ramifications provokes the poet's rebellion. Such, in a nutshell, is Mayakovsky's early creed, a variant of individualistic anarchism expressed in a suitably unique style.

A Cloud in Pants (1915) is the most characteristic long poem of Mayakovsky. Here primitive exuberance alternates with sophisticated satire and venomous hatred of the modern environment. The pattern is intricate; extremely individualistic notes are interwoven with social motives. This complexity is foreshadowed in the Prologue, wherein he "teases" the smug reader with the alternative of being now "ferocious," now "changing tones like the sky, irreproachably tender, not a male but a cloud in pants." The poet's "I" dominates the poem from the beginning to the end, varying in mood and key, the sardonically arrogant note prevailing. Thus: "I, insolent and caustic, shall satiate myself with mockery. There is not one white hair in my soul, nor any senile tenderness. Bethundering the world with the might of my voice, I march—handsome, twenty-two-years-old." Or, farther down: "Glorify me! I am no match for the great. I inscribe 'Nihil' over everything done before me." "I shall go away, and insert the sun as a monocle into my wide open eye. . . . Ahead of me I shall lead Napoleon on a chain, like a dog." Here and there megalomania gives place to humility and the groan of an aching heart. Mayakovsky, loather of sentimentalism and hackneyed words, holds his own even when he faces so ancient a theme as unrequited love. Old words and much-used similes he employs with ironic exaggeration that lends to his personal grief a Gargantuan aspect, the tragic mingling with the comic and tempered by it. When "Maria" rejects him, he telephones to his mother: "Hello! . . . Mama? Mama! Your son is superbly sick! Mama! He has a conflagration of the heart. . . . He has no place to go. Every word of his, even the jest which he belches through his singed mouth, is hurled out like a naked prostitute from a bawdy house on fire." Then he proceeds to picture the conflagration in his heart, with firemen in brass helmets and heavy boots scaling his ribs, and himself making a desperate and vain effort to "leap out of his heart." This method notwithstanding, Mayakovsky fails to hide the genuineness of his yearning pain.

Indeed, he is most genuine and convincing when he opens his heart and becomes "human—all-too-human." Pretensions are then discarded, obsessions of grandeur are replaced by the humble cry of a big, an "enormous" body which "at night craves to hide its resonance within something soft, womanly." His entreaties to Maria, despite all hyperboles, betray his helplessness before a primitive emotion. There is no mention of love, of moonlight and flowers, and the rest of the hateful heritage; his words and similes are heavy and coarse, but, as he says with a smirk: "When my voice bellows lewdly ... perhaps Jesus Christ smells the forget-me-nots of my soul." Modestly he admits that, unlike the genteel composer of sonnets for his beloved, he is "all flesh, all man—he begs for her body as Christians pray: 'Give us this day our daily bread.' " "Maria!" he cries: "Your name I dread to forget, as a poet is afraid to forget a certain in-the-pangs-of-night-born word, in majesty equal to god. Your body I shall guard and love, as a soldier hacked by the war, unwanted, nobody's, guards his only leg." Since Maria does not respond to his pleas, he "will once more, dark and downcast, take his heart, bedrip it with tears, and carry it as a dog carries into the kennel its paw run over by a train." Job-like, he proceeds to blaspheme, but less respectfully, threatening to knife "Mister God" "from here to Alaska." The "tetraptych" concludes in a minor note: "The universe sleeps, its huge ear resting on its paw with claws of stars."

Parallel with this personal lyricism, the poem contains a motive of rebellion. Mayakovsky addresses the "street thousands—students, prostitutes, contractors," not as a superior, but as one of the lowly, "vomited by a consumptive night into the palm of Moscow." He is a twentieth-century François Villon, a singer of the rabble, of criminals and harlots, of the miserable and the destitute. The poet, "a lip-shouting Zarathustra of today," he of "the most golden mouth, whose every word newbears the soul, angeldays the body," he calls upon the crowds to show self-respect: "You are not beggars, you dare not beg for alms!" He advises them that, though convicts and lepers, they are "purer than Venetian azure." They may be pockmarked and besmudged, yet "the sun would grow dim on beholding the gold quartz of their souls!" The poet himself, "derided by today's tribe like a long, scabrous anecdote," assures the masses that he is capable of perceiving ahead, where "men's docktailed eyes stop short." Indeed, he prophesies, proving wrong only by one year, "the advent of the year Sixteen, in the thorny crown of revolutions." Mayakovsky proclaims himself the "forerunner" of the pending event: "I am where there is pain—everywhere. On every drop of a flowing tear I have crucified myself." The "event" he describes graphically enough, allowing for the savage war censorship of 1915: "Suddenly both stormclouds and the other cloud folk raised an unheard-of racket in the sky, as though bloused workmen scurried, upon declaring a furious strike against heaven. Raging, thunder crept out from behind a cloud, saucily blew its gigantic nostrils, and for a second the skyey face twitched in the stern grimace of an iron Bismarck."

Unlike the majority of the Russian intelligentsia who had dreams of a gentle, fairy-tale transformation, Mayakovsky envisages the revolution as a bloody affair. He foresees another "General Galliffet come to shoot the rebels! Take the hands out your pockets, you strollers, pick up a stone, a knife, or a bomb, and he who has no hands let him come and butt with his forehead!" Parodying the New Testament, Mayakovsky roars: "Come ye who are hungry, sweaty, meek, soured in flea-ridden filth! Mondays and Tuesdays we shall color into holidays—with blood! ... And so that in the fever of cannonade flags may flutter, as on any decent holiday, lift higher, O lampposts, the gory corpses of shopkeepers!" Clearly, Mayakovsky's vision of the revolution did not go at the moment beyond riot, anarchy, and slaughter.

I have dwelt at some length on *A Cloud in Pants,* because this poem epitomizes Mayakovsky's art both before and after 1917. For although with the revolution he matured politically, and as a tribune of the people he began to write more simply, Mayakovsky remained essentially the same as a man and as a poet. This brings us back to the question of his style, which ought to be discussed, if only briefly.

By his upbringing and make-up Mayakovsky was an enemy of the social order as it existed up to 1917. He detested everything connected with it; above all, its aesthetics, in which he saw the reflection of its tyranny and smugness. From his very first attempt at writing he steadfastly eschewed the use of words that comprise the stock in trade of conventional poetry. In all his voluminous output you will not find a single worn epithet for the description of nature or man or emotions. When he does employ canned phrases, he obviously holds his tongue in his cheek, as some of the quoted excerpts may show. Yet Mayakovsky's rich and colorful (at times even gaudy) vocabulary has little if any of the *zaúm,* irrational, element introduced by the futurists. He does not coin entirely new words, but rather multiplies and variegates existing roots by means of the endless choice of prefixes and suffixes that makes the Russian speech so elastic, precise, and suggestive. By taking liberties with grammar and syntax, by the unexpected juxtaposition of sounds and words, he lends freshness and newness to otherwise familiar language. He does not hesitate to abbreviate or augment words, or to combine two into one for the sake of nuance and euphony, nor to change adverbs into adjectives, verbs into nouns, and *vice versa,* nor to omit prepositions when the meaning is clear without them, especially when their presence threatens cacophony. His language thus escapes being smooth and neat, calm and correct "like the pulse of a corpse," to use one of his characteristic similes. It is not the language of the salon or the study, but one of street harangue, and is therefore bold, irregular, trenchant, and laconic.

Similarly, in prosody Mayakovsky revolts against canonized aesthetics. The melodiousness of the Russian tonic-syllabic verse nauseated him by its trim regularity. His verse, not unlike Russian folk poetry, is based on the number of stressed syllables in a line, with no regard for the nonstressed syllables; this results in flexible tonality and greater freedom of rhythm. Coupled with metric irregularity is the typographic feature of broken lines. Mayakovsky writes not for silent reading, but for loud declamation. Not trusting punctuation marks, which he uses very sparingly, he directs the reader's intonation by making each line an accented unit, virtually a caesura. Accordingly, his line at times consists of one word. The lines I have quoted would have to be read differently if they were printed here as in the original. This passage, for instance, from page 70, appears thus:

> Maria!
> Your name I dread to forget,
> as a poet is afraid to forget
> a certain
> in-the-pangs-of-night-born word,
> in majesty equal to god.
> Your body
> I shall guard and love
> as a soldier
> backed by war,
> unwanted,
> nobody's,
> guards his only leg.

This rhythm became particularly apt during the revolutionary years, when Mayakovsky acted as a "drummer" (he drew endless sonorities out of *baraban,* the Russian word for drum), addressing himself to large masses, to marching soldiers. His celebrated "Left March" (1918), dedicated to the Red sailors, in which each of the four stanzes ends with the refrain

> Left!
> Left!
> Left!

was recited (and later, sung) collectively in pageants and processions, the marchers following the beats of the lines, as Mayakovsky meant them to be declaimed. His is, indeed, a revolutionary rhythm, dynamic and elemental, of a zigzaggy tempo.

Mayakovsky's verse, when not free or blank, is rhymed in the most whimsical way. He has discovered a wealth of consonant possibilities, for the most part unprecedented in Russian poetry. He alternates subtle inner rhymes with clusters of words combined to echo the ending of a previous line. Some of his rhyming tricks verge on puns, and make one question the poet's earnestness.

A more important feature of Mayakovsky's style is his metaphors. Here he manifestly differs from both realist and symbolist poets, for his images are neither of the everyday variety, like the former's, nor do they represent abstractions, like the latter's. In the language of the Schoolmen, he strives after *realiora*. He is never abstract, and even supernatural images he drags down to earth and renders concrete and sensory. At the same time, he clothes his metaphors in a hyperbolic form, deliberately, and often not without humor, exaggerating dimensions and concepts. The description of his heart on fire, quoted above, may illustrate the point. After 1917, especially in his *Mystery Bouffe* (1918), and in *150,000,000* (1920), Mayakovsky made abundant use of this hyperbolic style. The revolutionary upheaval, complicated by wars, invasions, the blockade, and their concomitant misery and suffering, heightened the tone of life, quickened its tempo—in a word, lent life a heroic style. Mayakovsky felt in his element, employing and even enhancing his hyperbolic method, now that his country and his people have made the improbable real by defeating seemingly insurmountable obstacles. There is elemental grandeur in the scene of his Unclean Ones storming the universe (*Mystery Bouffe*), or in his titanic Woodrow Wilson, personifying the capitalist order, and equally gargantuan Ivan, the collective embodiment of the victorious proletariat (*150,000,000*). The revolutionary period, its formative years, its groping efforts at destroying and building, its Homeric aspect, found a suitable poet in Mayakovsky.

It would be futile to search for Mayakovsky's indebtedness to other poets. He was not a man of books; traditions and clichés revolted him. There was no Russian poet, before him or during his lifetime, whom he even remotely resembled. It might be easier, indeed, to discover a kinship between Mayakovsky and certain poets of the Western world, specifically the *poètes maudits*. The term need not here be applied only to the French group of the Baudelaire-Rimbaud variety, but to all poets with whom Mayakovsky shared an extreme accentuation of the personal ego, a bent for the sublimation of base subjects and common "street" words, a fondness for new, striking forms and rhythms, and similar unorthodox leanings. This kinship is of a general nature, however. One may point out, in the same way, Mayakovsky's affinity for Verhaeren's note of urbanism, not forgetting how differently the two men treated city themes and voices. Mayakovsky's preoccupation with his self sounds often like an echo of Walt Whitman. Such of his verses as "Bethundering the world with the might of my voice, I march—handsome, twenty-two-years-old" bring to mind Whitman's "Song of Myself": "I celebrate myself, and sing myself ... I, now thirty-seven years old in perfect health ... ," or his line: "Of physiology from top to toe I sing." But again, there is only a casual resemblance between the unrhymed verses of the expansive democrat and the intricately rhymed lines of the intransigent revolutionary.[3]

─────────

[3] Professor G. R. Noyes, while reading the manuscript of this work, questioned "whether Severyanin and Mayakovsky, each with his rampant worship of his own ego, were influenced by Whitman." In my efforts to answer this pertinent question I have failed to find any data about Severyanin, but I have come upon two sources regarding Mayakovsky's relation to foreign poets: Chukovsky and Burlyuk.

In the Introduction to his new translation of *Leaves of Grass* (1935) Korney Chukovsky (b. 1882) wrote:

"In 1915, when I was working on my translations from Walt Whitman, Mayakovsky evinced considerable interest in his poetry. Mayakovsky was at that time very much impressed by the role of Whitman in the history of world poetry as a destroyer of Old-Testamental literary traditions, damned by the 'many-headed louse' of Philistia. ... Walt Whitman was dear to him as a forerunner."

Mayakovsky could have read Whitman in Balmont's translation and in the more robust version of Chukovsky. In his later recollections (*Repin. Gorky. Mayakovsky.*

An analysis of the huge output of Mayakovsky's pen and brush is beyond the scope of this essay. Leaving aside his numerous small pieces—lyrics, satires, marches, propaganda bits on various issues of the day, verses for children, essays and speeches—mention should be made of his large compositions. Prior to 1917 he published, besides *A Cloud in Pants*, a tragedy, *Vladimir Mayakovsky* (1912), two cycles of *War* (1914 and 1917), *Flute-Spine* (1916), *Man* (1916). The dominant motive during this phase is "I," "Mayakovsky," as exemplified in such themes and titles as "Today I am going to play on a flute. On my own spinal chord"; "To myself the beloved are these lines dedicated by the author"; "Mayakovsky's Nativity"; "Mayakovsky's Passions"; "Mayakovsky's Ascension"; "Maya-

Bryusov. 1940) Chukovsky offers additional details about Mayakovsky's attitude toward Whitman. The young Russian was particularly impressed, it appears, by what Chukovsky labels eccentricities, such as:
"Walt Whitman, a kosmos, of Manhattan the son,
   Turbulent, fleshy, sensual, eating, drinking and breeding . . ."
or:
"Divine am I inside and out, and I make holy whatever I touch or am touch'd from,
   The scent of these arm-pits aroma finer than prayer,
   This head more than churches, bibles, and all the creeds."
Mayakovsky reproached Chukovsky for his early versions of Whitman, which sounded too "bonbonily," too melodiously; he urged a "tougher, more rugged" version. Chukovsky was amazed at some of his suggested words and phrases: they were infinitely closer to the original than those of Chukovsky:
"Though not knowing the English original, Mayakovsky divined it as unerringly, and spoke of it with as firm assurance as if he were himself the author of those verses."
Mayakovsky read no foreign poets in the original. He depended on extant translations and on Burlyuk, of whom he wrote in an autobiographical sketch, "I Myself": "A superb friend. My real teacher. Burlyuk has made a poet out of me. He used to read to me Frenchmen and Germans." In answer to my inquiry, David Burlyuk informs me that among the poets from whom he translated passages for his "pupil and younger friend" were Homer, Vergil, Hugo, Baudelaire, Rimbaud, Moréas, Corbière, Paul Fort, Maeterlinck, Verhaeren, "and many others, also 'Germans,' especially Rainer Maria Rilke." In regard to Whitman, Burlyuk states categorically that he "had *no* influence on Mayakovsky." Burlyuk resents Chukovsky's notion that Mayakovsky could have been affected by "Whitman—calm and balanced like a stuffed fish (What is the good of a poet who does not summon you to change life, does not explode things, does not wallop you in the jaw, but only emotionalizes 'democratically' and professorializes?)."
There is an interesting article on "Mayakovsky and the Literature of the West" by A. V. Fedorov in a collection of papers on *Vladimir Mayakovsky*, published in 1940 by the Institute of Literature of the U.S.S.R. Academy of Sciences.

kovsky in Heaven"; "Mayakovsky to the Ages." Along with this motif the poet voices his disgust with the world as it is; he hurls invectives and threats at the smug and stagnant social order, but he sees no way out, and consequently sounds a rather dismal note.

As already noted, Mayakovsky wrote about nine-tenths of his work after 1917. During the last thirteen years of his life he grew to his full stature. The revolution and its multiple tasks filled his void, and gave meaning and contents to his resentments, grievances, and vague aspirations. His style, too, matured, became free from obscurity, from trickery, from an excessive burden of similes, and from dispensable coarseness. A style of the street, it now represented not the street of strutting philistines, criminals, pimps, and prostitutes, but the streets and squares of a country jolted from age-old apathy to a desperate struggle for its existence and a finer life. Mayakovsky was proud to consider himself a worker, a sharer in the national travail, never too squeamish about using his pen or brush or voice for "propaganda." "I feel as if I were a Soviet workshop, manufacturing happiness. I do not care to be plucked after a day of toil, like a flower off the meadow.... I want the Gosplan [State Planning Commission] to sweat while discussing the assignment of my year's tasks. I want the pen to be put on the same footing with the bayonet. I want Stalin in the name of the Politbureau to present reports on the production of verse along with reports on pig iron and steel."

During these arduous years, in the rare moments of leisure he could find, what with his daily "attacks" waged against the enemies of the new order and his frequent travels at home and abroad, Mayakovsky managed to compose a few long poems and plays, in addition to his shorter writings. One of the plays, *Mystery Bouffe*, was in verse, a heroic rhapsody of the revolution. The two prose plays, *The Bedbug* (1928) and *The Bathhouse* (1930), castigated philistine smugness that began to raise its head in the "normal" years following the civil wars. Among his travel poems, the cycle on the United States (1925–1926) is noteworthy: he caught. the rhythm of the country, mingling his admiration for its tech-nological advancement with his revulsion from the wastage and cruelty of its economic order. Of the long poems of that period, mention has been made of *150,000,000,* with its theme of the clash between Wilson, personifying Western capitalism, and the peasant Ivan, who symbolizes the Russian masses. *Of This* (1923) sounded like a relapse into preoccupation with his self and a futile quest of completeness in love. Unlike this poem, his *'Tis Good!* (1927) was exuberant and social in motive, voicing a militant opti-mism about the land of Soviets. His most ambitious long poem is *Vladimir Ilich Lenin* (1924), written shortly after the death of the man. Here the poet's ever-present note of personal lyricism merges with the broad notes of a national epic. Kalinin's announcement of Lenin's death to the Congress of Soviets, and the scene of the funeral, are among Mayakovsky's highest achievements. There is not one loud word or obvious emotionalism, and the author's unwonted reserve intensifies the tragic sense of the moment.

The life and work of Mayakovsky have been an open book, largely owing to the extrovert nature of his verse. He has turned himself inside out, flaunted intimate details of his past and present, painted a self-portrait of full length and depth. Everything about him, as suggested previously, was elemental and elementary, there-fore simple and lucid. Everything, except for one thing: his end. The public was shocked and dumbfounded when on April 14, 1930, Mayakovsky shot himself.

The premature death of a poet had become, one might say, a tradition in Russia. One need only mention Pushkin and Lermon-tov (1814–1841), killed in duels at the age of thirty-seven and twenty-seven, respectively; then, omitting other examples and taking into account only the first dozen years after the revolution, we come on the execution of the thirty-five-year-old Gumilyov, the deaths from physical exhaustion and mental apathy of Blok (aged forty-one) and Khlebnikov (thirty-seven), the suicides of Yesenin (thirty), Kuznetsov (twenty), and Mayakovsky (thirty-seven). All these died primarily because of failure to adjust themselves to their environment. The death of Mayakovsky, however, came as a surprise, for he had given no obvious signs of maladjustment.

Quite to the contrary. Five years previously, Yesenin, a popular imagist poet, cut his wrists and hanged himself, a victim of drunken debauches, ill-digested fame, and notoriety, and of an ideally mismatched marriage (to Isadora Duncan). Dipping the pen into the blood of his slashed wrists (there was a shortage of ink at the time), Yesenin scribbled a note that ended with the lines:

> In this life 'tis nothing new to die,
> Nor is it, of course, more novel to live.

Mayakovsky felt a need of counteracting Yesenin's gesture. In a later essay, "How to Make Verses," reminiscent of Poe's would-be confession of how he wrote his "Raven," Mayakovsky explained his methods and moods in composing the poem "To Sergey Yesenin" (1926), as well as his main motive. Yesenin's final lines, he was convinced, precisely because they were *verse* (italics his), "would draw many vacillating citizens into the noose and in front of the revolver muzzle." Although Mayakovsky's poem was written in his usual bantering tone, one feels keenly its warmth of emotion and the personal concern of a poet chiding his brother for a fainthearted act. He admits that "this time is rather hard for the pen," but then, he asks, "where, when, what great man has chosen a worn and easy path?" Life must be remade—such is the task of the moment. He ends with a paraphrase of Yesenin's lines:

> In this life
>   'tis not hard to die.
> To mold life
>   is far more difficult.

This sentiment deceived the public with respect to Mayakovsky's state of mind. He probably deceived himself into believing that he was perfectly at home and at ease under the Soviet regime. There is no question about the sincerity and loyalty of his attitude toward the new order. His service to the "attacking class" was both wholehearted and effective, the latter merit being acknowledged even by Lenin,[4] who personally failed to appreciate Mayakovsky's poetry. But neither can there be any question about the inner split that he experienced most of the time, even—or especially—when protesting his buoyant faith the loudest. For him the difficulty of "molding life" consisted in harmonizing the moods and whims of the bohemian individualist he had been up to 1917, with the convictions of the disciplined Bolshevik he valiantly strove to be thereafter. His last poems, especially *Of This* and *In Full Voice* (1930), show the cumulative intensity of his inner contradictions, which proved catastrophic. He tells us that again and again he endeavored to stifle the individualist in him, that he "put his foot on the throat of his song." The half-smothered note persisted, however, as an overtone, and insinuated itself now and then as a moan. I refer to such recurrent motives as loneliness, suicide, unrequited love, being misunderstood and underrated by his contemporaries. Here belongs his masterly *Jubilean,* wherein he takes the bronze Pushkin for a stroll, after removing him from his pedestal in the famous Moscow square. In a half-jesting tone, behind which one is aware of his profound pain, he pours his heart out to his great predecessor, another rebel who smashed his head

---

[4] In the *Izvestiya* for March 5, 1922, Mayakovsky published his "Outsitters," a satire on bureaucratic methods of endless sessions and discussions of trivial matters. The next day Lenin mentioned this satire in a public speech:

"I do not belong to the admirers of his poetic talent, though I fully admit my incompetence in that field. But it is a long time since I have experienced such pleasure from the political and administrative points of view. In his poem Mayakovsky makes deadly fun of 'meetings,' and ridicules communists who sit and oversit in sessions. I do not know about the poetry, but I vouch that politically this is absolutely correct. We do find ourselves in the position (and one must say, a silly position it is) of men who are perpetually in session, composing plans, commissions—to infinity."

Needless to say, Lenin's pragmatic praise was of inestimable encouragement to the erstwhile futurist, now "a sewer cleaner and water carrier, mobilized and summoned by the Revolution."

against the wall of environment. Mayakovsky confides to Pushkin that soon he too will be dead, and then their names will stand not so far apart in the alphabet of the great.

The immediate causes of his suicide were apparently a combination of illness (lingering grippe), loneliness, persecution, and what he regarded as unrequited love. Although he had parted company with futurism and LEF, and had joined the arch-orthodox RAPP, certain zealots continued to taunt him and to doubt his devotion. A few days before his death, he declared publicly: "They hang so many dogs on me, and accuse me of so many sins . . . that at times I feel like going off somewhere for a couple of years, only not to listen to abuse." Such intimate friends as Aseyev bitterly recall the nagging and sarcastic remarks Mayakovsky had to suffer from those little Torquemadas. As to the poet's known love for the wife of a close comrade and collaborator, his farewell poem contains a sufficient hint that all was not smooth in their relationship. The final message follows, in part:

Already past one.
    You must be in bed.
Across the night
    the milky way
        a silver Oka River.
I am in no hurry
    and am not going
        to wake you
with special telegrams
    and disturb you.
As they say,
    the incident is closed.
Love boat smashed against environment.
You and I
    are quits.

No need of listing
mutual hurts
    sorrows
        and grievances.
Look
    how peaceful the world.
Night
    has imposed on the sky
        a starry contribution.
At just such hours
    you rise up
        and speak
    to ages,
        to history,
            to creation.

Some of the puns and nuances are lost in translation; only the raw directness and unhackneyed phraseology may be conveyed.

In the final version the lines "You and I/are quits" were changed to "Life and I/are quits." Mayakovsky was fastidious in his last hours, and tried to make his death as neat and free from scandal as possible. In a letter addressed before his death to "Mama, sisters, comrades," he apologized for what he was about to do, and ended with the request: "Please don't gossip. The deceased disliked that awfully."

Let us resist, therefore, the temptation to gossip. It is clear— "clear to the point of hallucination," as Mayakovsky would say— that the poet was not a monochrome (Soviet writers prefer the word "monolith"). His inner conflicts and contradictions made his life a tragedy; but they were hardly detrimental to his poetry. The two—or more—selves of this monumental child of nature were voiced forcefully and with unique skill. Regardless of his emotional "deviations," Mayakovsky's work will live chiefly as an expression of the Will to Revolution and, therefore, as most representative of contemporary Russia. This consideration justifies the lengthy treatment allotted him in this essay.

Aseyev.—Nikolay Aseyev (b. 1889) is the chief survivor of the once-domineering futurism. In 1939, the twenty-fifth anniversary of his first book of poems, *Nocturnal Flute,* was celebrated throughout the Union, and he was decorated with the Order of Lenin (a *coup de grâce* to futurism as an expression of extreme individualism and iconoclasm). There is hardly an article about Aseyev that fails to mention his closeness to Mayakovsky. Indeed, Aseyev belonged to the small circle of Mayakovsky's congenial companions (it is doubtful whether the late poet had real friends). In his *Jubilean,* Mayakovsky confides to Pushkin that Aseyev is not bad: "He has my knack." Aseyev has written some valuable critical notes and reminiscences about Mayakovsky. In 1940 appeared his *Mayakovsky Starts Off,* "a novel in verse" about the late poet, who is pictured from intimate angles in a rhythm and vocabulary closely resembling his own.

The frequent juxtaposition of the two poets is damaging to
Aseyev, because it brings into relief his relative inferiority. In com-
paring them, one cannot escape the conclusion that Aseyev is a
pale reflection of Mayakovsky, that he is less original, less vigorous,
less penetrating, less memorable—in a word, a lesser Mayakovsky.
Aseyev is by no means a slavish imitator of Mayakovsky, and were
it not for the coupling of the two names one would value Aseyev
for his own unquestionable merits. His range is wide, his form
varies from regular meter to futuristic broken lines and rhythms,
and his vocabulary is both fresh and clear, never displaying the
extreme coinages of some of his early fellow futurists. Aseyev is
primarily a lyricist, a recorder of his emotions and observations
with a gentle directness that is free both from sentimentality and
from the once fashionable bolshevist Spartanism. This lyricism
he combines with a social note, blending the two elements imperceptibly and synthetically, even in such of his ambitious epics as
The Twenty-six Murdered Commissars and *Semyon Proskakov.*
He avoids generalities and abstractions; his portraits and landscapes are specific and concrete. In his romantic collection, *Won-
derful Things,* he uses such visual terms as these:

> You have seen
>   how to the sky
>   an arrow soars up,
> how beams are hewn,
>   laths are planed;
> you have seen
>   how horses gnaw their bits,
> how cement is mixed,
>   how tanks snort,
> how aeroplanes
>   glide on wings,
> and their four-motor
>   shadow floats—
> a reliable protection
>   of the Soviet land.

He speaks plainly and directly, even when he betrays his old penchant for futuristic form; hence, his wide popularity. In paraphrasing Mayakovsky, Aseyev modestly states:

> In my poetic travail
>   I flounder at words,
>   and words come forth tight,
>   but I am glad
>   that they are in demand,
>   like steel,
>   like machines,
>   like coal.

PASTERNAK

Another poet linked with the futurists is Boris Pasternak (b. 1890), a veritable poet for poets. There is hardly one critic who questions the superb quality of Pasternak's art, his originality, the striking freshness of his imagery and similes, the simplicity and, at the same time, subtlety of his words—ordinary conversational speech which acquires under his pen unexpected meaning and precision of shades. For years he was classified as a futurist, a label he bore indifferently, as he would any other label. Pasternak is primarily a lyricist, a self-centered contemplator, incapable of joining wholeheartedly any group or movement. The only trait that lends him kinship with the futurists is the involved syntax of his verse, which produces "estrangement" and difficulty of understanding, so dear to the heart of a formalist. Otherwise, he indulges in no neologisms, his rich and unusual rhythms are regular, and his amazingly skillful and original rhymes are free from trickery. Pasternak has influenced a number of poets, but he remains essentially inimitable, since it is not so much the form that makes his poetry distinct as his way of seeing the world, and this of course reflects his own exclusive personality. The son of a well-known painter, he grew up in a highly cultivated environment, acquired a broad erudition, and developed catholic interests. Thus, in addition to being well

versed in literature, music, and painting, he studied philosophy
at the universities of Moscow and Marburg. In reading Pasternak,
one is aware of his extraordinary intellectual baggage, though it
never protrudes from his delicately intimate lines. He strikes you
with the novelty of his approach to life, to nature, to everyday
object and scene. You get the impression of listening to a man
of a different planet, who wonderingly contemplates our life for
the first time, and is therefore utterly innocent of hackneyed images and threadbare comparisons. Here, for example, is one of his
"Springs," translated by George Reavey (*Soviet Literature: An
Anthology*, 1933):

> Spring! I am from the street, where the poplars stand amazed,
> Where the distance takes fright, where the house fears to fall,
> Where the air is all blue, like the linen bundle
> Of a patient just discharged from the hospital.
>
> Where the evening's vacant, like an interrupted story,
> Left in an asterisk without any sequel
> To the suspense of a thousand clamoring eyes,
> Bereft of expression grown deeply abysmal.

The difficulty of grasping Pasternak's meaning at once is usually rewarded by the ultimate pleasure of seeing with his eyes and
hearing with his ears. Thus, you may enjoy the steppe at night,
and its glistening unpaved road, in which stars are reflected, after
you wade through the cool, rhythmic, somewhat obscure lines, the
atmosphere of which can hardly be conveyed in translation:

> Century-old midnight stands by the road,
> Sprawls on the road with its stars,
> And to get across beyond the hedge
> One cannot without tramping the universe.

Nor can my literal translation suggest the joyous sounds of a
piano in the lines:

> The flock of the claviature I fed from the hand,
> To the flapping of wings, cackling and fuss.

Pasternak hardly ever gives the impression of a labored effort at saying things differently. He inspires you with confidence that he feels precisely as his verse sounds; when, for example, he tells us that his beloved

> Has entered with a chair,
> Reached for my life, as though from a shelf,
> And shaken off its dust.

Or when he describes a thunderstorm in the country:

> And then summer took his farewell
> Of the flag station. Doffing his cap,
> Thunder took that night as a souvenir
> A hundred blinding snapshots.

Or a gentle summer shower:

> Rather from sleep than from the roofs; rather
> Forgetful than timid,
> Jibbed the little shower by the door,
> And it smelled of a wine cork.

Pasternak has often been reproached for his aloofness from social questions. "What's the millennium, dear people, outdoors at the moment?" asks the poet with wide-open eyes. The luxury of detachment can be ill afforded in the dynamic life of Soviet Russia. Pasternak is heartily in accord with the new order, and he has made several attempts to attune his lyre to the demands of the time. In prose and in poetry he has produced work dealing with revolutionary experience, notably his *1905*. It is quite evident, however, that in these efforts Pasternak is outside his ken.

Of late he has engaged in translations from foreign poets, such as French symbolists and poets of Soviet national minorities, the Georgians, for example. In 1940, he completed a masterly translation of Shakespeare's *Hamlet*. Whether this later activity of his spells a temporary escape from his conflicting urges, time may tell. Pasternak's translations from the Georgian are worthy of his talent, and have aroused public endorsement and emulation. A movement was launched among Soviet poets to master at least one other language from among the hundred-odd tongues of the Union, with the aim of transmitting to one another the poetic wealth of the component nationalities. Pavlo Tychina (b. 1891), the leading Ukrainian poet, has been studying Georgian and Yiddish. His example has been followed by a number of well-known poets who have begun to learn and to translate some Soviet language not their own. Among them are such Russians as Tikhonov, Aseyev, Prokofyev (b. 1900), Antokolsky (b. 1896), Golodny (b. 1903), Lugovskoy (b. 1901), Svetlov (b. 1903), Isakovsky (b. 1900), Surkov (b. 1899), the Ukrainian Bazhanov (b. 1904), the Georgian Gaprindashvili (b. 1890), and many others.

TIKHONOV

Like Pasternak, Nikolay Tikhonov (b. 1896) has influenced many of the younger poets by the form of his verse, particularly by his *Ballads*. These were published in the mid-'twenties, and dealt chiefly with Tikhonov's experiences as a hussar in the World War and as a Jack-of-all-trades in the formative years of the Soviet state, carpentering, teaching, acting, fighting the Whites—in a word, leading a life common to the great majority of Soviet authors. Though imbued with the romance of war and revolution, Tikhonov's ballads and lyrics had a terseness and precision that placed them apart from the hackneyed effusions of the moment. The bloodiest and most fantastic details of his poems (and nearly every one of them has a story to tell) possess the intensity of reserve. In the following twelve lines, for instance, he gives the essence of those years of dread and wonder that inspired his muse:

> Fire, the rope, bullet and axe,
> Like flunkeys bowed and followed us;
> And in every drop a deluge was dormant,
> Mountains grew forth out of small pebbles,

> And within a twig crushed by the foot
> Rustled black-armed forests.
> Untruth ate and drank with us,
> Church bells droned by force of habit,
> Coins had lost their weight and ring,
> And children were not scared of corpses.
> It was then for the first time we learned
> Beautiful words, bitter and cruel.

Tikhonov shows traces of indebtedness to the acmeists. He doubtless profited from their best principles—clarity, concreteness of the images, severe precision. "Simple as iron nails," he recommended himself, as a result of special training:

> Life taught with oar and rifle,
> With a stout breeze across my shoulders;
> Lashed with a knotted cord,
> To render me poised and nimble,
> Simple—like iron nails.

Though not a communist, and often in bitter opposition to Party policies, Tikhonov had declared, in his "simple" way, that Soviet Russia is for him "the only Russia," which he "loves firmly and is ready to stand by." Despite his occasional deviations into formalism, he has always shown an intense concern about the world outside of his personal self. In his lyrics and ballads, in his stories and novels (written in a robust and brilliant prose), and in his latest cycle of *Poems about Europe,* Tikhonov succeeds in presenting a composite portrait of his generation. He shows us not only Russia in war, revolution, famine, and plague; he knows Western Europe intimately enough to portray it during 1914–1918 (notably in his novel, *War*), and in the years of alleged peace which passeth all understanding, between the two World Wars. In the cycle of poems written after his travels in the west shortly before the Second World War, one feels the stifling air of fear and suspense that hovers over the cities and plains of the continent. Yet, as a citizen of the land of optimism and faith in the future, Tikhonov does not permit himself the luxury of despair. In the grim poem, "Anti-Gas," he addresses the hideous gas mask, whose "clammy rubber, tightly stretched over Europe's head," deadens laughter, the rustle of forests, and the swish of grass. He is certain, however, that the reign of that mask cannot endure. For surely it was not for this that "man went to battle on the boulevards of tempestuous Paris," that English miners "swore their oaths," and Spaniards "bore dynamite beneath their rags," that men of Germany were "tortured in·the dark of dungeons," that Albania's heroes "died as dies a torch," and Abyssinians "shared their last drop of water with Italy's deceived riflemen." He refused to believe in the triumph of the horrible sack that "has stolen men's fine features." A day shall come when this mask, "invented on a sleepless night by a chemist who was haunted by the growls of the age," will be stuffed with straw and nailed to the outside of our houses:

> You will hang, a target for children,
> Bondman of the last cruelty.

> I shall be an old man, and come up to you.
> The sun will be setting beyond the Neva,
> And near by a song will flare up
> And touch our windswept cheeks.

IMAGISTS

The noisiest offspring of symbolism—or rather of its derivative, futurism—appeared under the name of imagism or imaginism. Its first "Declaration" was published in 1919, and was signed by the poets Yesenin, Ivnev, Mariengof (b. 1897), Shershenevich, and by some painters. In the rasping boastfulness of its tone, as well as in its cavalier contempt for other schools, the Declaration sounded like an echo of the early manifestoes of Russian futurism, herein announced as having become academic and dogmatic, and having expired (literally: "croaked"—*izdokh*). It proclaimed the image as the only important element in art, as "the naphthalene that preserves a work from the moths of time." Subject matter, content, was branded as "the vermiform appendix of art," silly and senseless in any artistic production.

Yesenin, Mariengof, Shershenevich were the most gifted poets of the imagist school, and also its leading theoreticians. In the latter capacity they contradicted one another, and on occasion even themselves. Shershenevich, whose Protean virtuosity has already been noted, easily passed from the role of a champion of futurism to that of its gravedigger and the protagonist of imagism. In justice to Shershenevich it should be pointed out that as early as 1915 he declared himself to be "primarily an imagist," explaining his adherence to futurism by the fact that its "theory corresponded most closely to his views on the role of the image." It was in the same year, 1915, that Zinaida Vengerova published a paper on "English Futurists," in which she recorded a conversation with Ezra Pound, of imagist fame and vorticist notoriety, and more recently branded as a champion of Mussolini. Pound showed her the proofs of *Blast*, the first symposium of the vorticists about to come out in print, and permitted Vengerova to publish some of its horrendous tenets. These made an impression on those of Russia's young poets whose preoccupation with images found not enough elbow room among either the symbolists or the futurists. Four years later Shershenevich discarded the futurist compromise, and launched the imagist "movement," the last and ultimate word in poetry.[5]

---

[5] The limited scope of this study has not permitted the use of a comparative method, however tempting it has been to draw parallels between Russian rebels in poetry and their Western brethren. A brief reference to Marinetti was all that I found to be expedient in connection with the discussion of futurism (p. 9, fn. 5). As for imagism, its short history is probably known to English-speaking readers, since the movement was inaugurated and championed by English and American poets. The American, Ezra Pound, who joined the Poets' Club organized a year earlier in London by T. E. Hulme, was the first to apply the term "imagists" to his group. In the January, 1913, issue of *Poetry* (Chicago) Pound undertook to explain the "four cardinal principles" of imagism. The first was directness in treating the "thing"; the second, precision of the word; the third, "sequence of the musical phrase" in rhythm; the fourth principle demanded conformity to the "doctrine of the image," but this doctrine, Pound admitted with a coquettish smirk, had "not been defined for publication, as it does not concern the public, and would provoke

The place of images in art has been recognized for as long a time as art has existed. The imagists burst through an open door, their only claim to innovation lying in the emphasis they put on the paramount and well-nigh exclusive value of the image, on its alleged autonomy. Here Shershenevich goes farther than his fellow imagists. He insists on the "self-aim," the "autocracy" of the image. As against Yesenin, Mariengof, and other brethren, who regard the poem as an organism, an organic unity of images, Shershenevich insists on the independence of each image and its self-sufficiency. He is "deeply convinced" that his poems and those of other imagists can be read "with equal success" backward, just as

useless discussion." He condescended, however, to cast a pearl of an aphorism, of which he thought well enough to quote it in *Blast:* "An image is that which presents an intellectual and emotional complex in an instant of time." Another of his pontifical pearls was: "It is better to present one Image in a lifetime than to produce voluminous works."

In 1914, Ezra Pound published the first anthology of the imagists. Among its contributors were Richard Aldington, F. S. Flint, James Joyce, Ford Madox Hueffer; of American poets, aside from Pound, there were Amy Lowell, H. D. (Mrs. Aldington), William Carlos Williams. There was enough freshness and talent in the anthology to produce a favorable impression on the public. The danger of success prompted Pound to withdraw from the group and to join the vaguer and more iconoclastic group of "vorticists," in whose shrieking quarterly, *Blast* (it lasted for two issues), he took an active part.

Meanwhile Amy Lowell assumed the role of high priestess, and what with the generous "imagist dinners" she gave, and her energy and persistence in recruiting members, the group grew in numbers, and was represented in three more yearly anthologies (1915, 1916, 1917). To be sure, some of the "members" were of doubtful allegiance: D. H. Lawrence, for example. As to John Gould Fletcher, we are told by Pound that he "resisted imagism, but could not resist Amygism"; so Fletcher joined. The imagist "credo" announced in the 1915 anthology was less pretentiously esoteric than Ezra Pound's revelations, and might appeal to any good poet who had no objections to such principles as the employment of the exact word, the creation of new rhythms for new moods, freedom in the choice of subject, "hard and clear" poetry as against blurred and vague generalities, and "concentration." In 1917, Amy Lowell proclaimed the "end of the movement." Apparently the basic ideas of imagism had spread widely enough to make the existence of a separate "movement" unnecessary. Yet in 1930 an *Imagist Anthology* was published in New York and London which included all the leading early members of the Amy Lowell group (Miss Lowell was no longer alive).

Like the Russian futurists and Marinetti, the Russian imagists owed to their Anglo-American counterpart no more than the name and the general line it suggests, as a starting point.

A detailed account of Anglo-American imagists may be found in Glenn Hughes's *Imagism and the Imagists,* Stanford University Press, 1931.

imagist paintings may hang upside down, presumably "with equal success." In his war against content, Shershenevich is likewise more intransigent. He rejects Mariengof's dictum: ". . . art is form. Content is one of form's parts. The whole is beautiful only when each one of its parts is beautiful. There can be no beautiful form without beautiful content. Depth of the content is the synonym of beauty." Shershenevich demands the "victory of the image over sense and the liberation of the word from content"; "the image must devour the sense." Hence his campaign against grammar, specifically against verbs and prepositions. Hence the word is at best an accessory: "The word is the ass that brings the Christ of the image into the Jerusalem of understanding." Hence, likewise: "The word upside down—that is the most natural position of the word, out of which a new image must be born."

Even sharper are the ideological discrepancies of the *maîtres* of imagism. Writing during the critical, formative years of the Soviet Union, these poets could hardly remain "above the battle"; they had to present some face to a public that had been roused from apathy and indifferentism. The imagists floundered, hemmed and hawed, and knocked their heads against one another's. Yesenin's rustic mysticism, Mariengof's suburban cynicism, Shershenevich's facile eclecticism clashed and collided amusingly. Reproached for contradictions, they tried to make the best of the situation by priding themselves on being contradictory. Were they mystics or realists? Both, asserted Mariengof: "For in the last account any mysticism, if it is not sheer charlatanism, is real, and any realism, if it is not commonplace naturalism, is mystic." Being more erudite and clever than his fellow imagists, Shershenevich faced a greater number of contradictions and pitfalls, and he tried to dodge them by coquettishly spurning logic and consistency. In all probability it was he who inserted in the "Declaration" the final paragraph, which relegated the task of formulating the philosophy of imagism to anybody who cared to undertake it. In his signed pamphlet, characteristically named $2 \times 2 = 5$, he engages in a polemic against all and sundry, and at times casts common sense and logic to the winds. He refuses to be dragged into the revolutionary struggle, for to him "the history of the whole proletariat, the whole history of mankind, is only an episode in comparison with the history of the development of the image." In one place he claims that "imagism has a quite definite philosophical ground (*obosnovaniye*)," but he fails to explain what he means by this "ground," unless it be this rather vague boast: "Imagism contains the birth of a new, classless, all-human idealism of the harlequin order." He endeavors to make clear the position of imagism with respect to its parents, symbolism and futurism, but here too he indulges in glittering generalities. He accuses symbolism of "philistine individualism," and of getting "stuck" in "philosophical transcendentalism of the past," while futurism he derides for its "philistine communism" and for stopping short before "the swamp of contemporaneity" despite its "nominal affirmation of the future." Wherein imagism differs from these schools is not quite clear, since both of them, especially symbolism, paid lavish tribute to the image, and again, both of them, particularly futurism, enlarged the medium by neologisms and inroads into grammar and prosody. There is little beyond bombast and fog in such assertions of Shershenevich as: "Imagism is the first thunderpeal of a universal spiritual revolution," or: "Imagism is a crusade toward the Jerusalem of Joy, where laughter slumbers in the Lord's tomb. Cognition is reached not by means of thinking but through tactility, in the same way as 'spring grabbles the body of the earth with blue brooks.'" Nor do we gain any clearer understanding of the position of imagism from his crowning aphorism: "Symbolism worshiped the gods of past eternity; futurism was destroying them; imagism is creating new deities, itself being first among them." Here and there Shershenevich makes light of his statements, exploding such nihilistic petards as: "Poetry's chief magnificent law is 'There are no laws whatever,'" or: "One must know less! Such is the principle of a genuine master poet, or, more correctly: One must know only that which one must know." Afraid lest he "swim into the backwater of sense and 'deep ideas,'" he winds up his discourse appropriately enough: "Thus I pick up the reins of my disheveled thoughts, and speed into nowhere my charlatanish charabanc."

For five or six years the imagists made themselves felt in Soviet life and literature. They had their own café in Moscow, their writings and public readings enjoyed a considerable response, and in the years of dire shortage in paper and printing facilities they managed to get published.[6] Two reasons may be offered for the quick, and brief, success of the imagists. They appeared on the stage at the low ebb of the revolution, when the military communism of the civil war period was giving place to the "breathing spell" of the NEP. The new bourgeoisie, the Nepmen audience, found the imagist verses more titillating to their jaded taste than the "regular" verse of the proletarian poets, or that of the futurists, which though "irregular" had become for the most part unequivocally pro-Bolshevik. In the second place, despite the charlatanism

---

[6] Particularly during the years 1920–1921, the number of imagist books and booklets of poetry was relatively higher than that of any other group. This is difficult to understand, in view of the fact that all publications had to receive paper and printing permits from the State Publishing House. The following letter of Lunacharsky (*Izvestiya*, April 14, 1921) illustrates the dexterity of the imagists as well as some of the awkward situations the tolerant ("spineless"—to his party comrades) Commissar of Education had to face:

"Quite a long time ago I agreed to be honorary president of the All-Russian Union of Poets, but only very recently was I able to become acquainted with some of the books published by members of that Union, among these *Golden Boiling Water,* by Yesenin, Mariengof, and Shershenevich.

"These books, as well as others published of late by the so-called Imagists, present a malicious outrage against their own gifts, against humaneness, and against present-day Russia.

"These books have been appearing illegally, that is to say, the paper and press have been obtained unlawfully, without the knowledge of the State Publishing House.

"The authorities have resolved to investigate the matter, and to indict those who were instrumental in the publication and spread of these disgraceful books.

"Since the Union of Poets failed to protest against this prostitution of talent . . . I hereby publicly announce my resignation as president of the Union."

of their prose declarations and the $2 \times 2 = 5$ logic of their theoretical efforts, the imagists were, on the whole, poets of talent, and their poems, however rich in images, were seldom devoid of content, Shershenevich's doctrine notwithstanding. One may add that their popularity with the piquancy-seeking audiences was due in part to the deliberate coarseness of their epithets and images. In his boldest similes and street words, Mayakovsky appeared as a genteel maiden in the light of the allusions of Shershenevich and Mariengof. Even the gentle Yesenin forced himself to appear rough and common, particularly in his last phase, the "Moscow Barroom" period.

Here is a sample of Shershenevich's imagery:

> With the ladles of lines one cannot scoop
> The cesspool of my soul.
> I say my prayers to the gambling-house queen of hearts,
> And the ikons I drag to the wrecking dump.
> An obscenely embroidered inscription
> I turn into a sacred psalm.
>
> Unbuttoned is my mouth, like a slit in the pants.
> And when from midnight's brow drips the sweat of a star,
> My noddle serves as a night lodging
> For all pilgrims of the Jerusalem of twaddle.
> ... Upon completing my work, denunciatory, hard,
> After heart-to-heart chats with folks,
> I seem to myself as a piece of paper
> Thrown into the water closet.

Anatol Mariengof's cold, intellectual verses are a curious mixture of the lofty and the base. He combines revolutionary pathos with callous sadism, sprinkling his gory dish with a goodly dose of blasphemy. He dreams of world revolution in terms of an itinerant meat grinder, passing "from Moscow to Berlin, Budapest, and Rome." Death and anarchy are emblazoned on his banner, he spurns love and pity, he raves about "pounds of human flesh," "lorries of children's bones—sugar lumps in a mortar," "lips avidly clinging to steaming wounds," "the earth like a butcher's apron, soaked in human blood." The bloodthirsty anarchist spits into Jehovah's "idiotic eye," recrucifies Christ, and strolls in the streets of Moscow arm in arm with Barabbas, Herod, Cain, and others of that kidney. In his skillfully composed *Yav'* ("Actuality"), he chants:

> We are ruffling the dry soil by its tufts,
> Holiness we lash with a whistling whip,
> And Christ's emaciated body
> We stretch on the Cheka[7] rack.
>
> Come now, come, forgive us sinners,
> Save us as you saved the sinner at Golgotha.
> Your blood, your blood furiously
> We splash out of the washbowl.
>
> I cry: "Mary, Mary, see whom you bore in your womb.
> I might have kissed the dust of your feet for an abortion."

Mariengof attempts to give the reason for the "copulation of the clean and unclean" in imagist poetry:

Why does Yesenin's sun "grow cold like a puddle ponded by a gelding," and his dawn "raise its tail cowlike over the grove"? . . .
One of the poet's aims is to arouse in the reader a maximum of inner tension. Into the palm of the reader's receptivity he must thrust as deeply as possible the splinter of an image. The crossing of the clean and unclean serves to sharpen the splinters with which the compositions of modern imagist poetry bristle in due measure.

Yesenin.—Yesenin's (1895–1925) allegiance to the imagists should be taken less seriously than even that of Mayakovsky to the futurists. For Mayakovsky did introduce and practice a number of poetic innovations in form and substance that might be labeled futuristic. As for Sergey Yesenin's poetry, it defies all -isms; when good, it is just good poetry, in regular and occasionally varying metric verse, in rhymed lyrics or in long blank-verse poems

---

[7] The dreaded Commission for the suppression of counterrevolution.

like *Pugachov*. Only occasionally does he make one aware of imagist trickery, and then his lines are overladen with similes and charged with labored coarseness. Otherwise his wealth of images merits the label of "imagism" no more than does that of Homer or the Russian heroic ballads, the *byliny*. Yesenin is nearer to the symbolists, except for their aristocraticism and cosmopolitan urbanity, than he is to any other modern school. Yesenin is an autochthonous Russian peasant; this fact accounts for the fundamental characteristics of his poetry. The pungent aroma of rural Russia permeates his verse, its imagery as much as its ideology, and no one illustrates the absurdity of Shershenevich's separation of image from content more brilliantly than Yesenin.

Brought up in a conservative and extremely religious household of Ryazan peasants, Yesenin was never able to shake off the world outlook he had absorbed from his birth. (He came to grief when he tried to do so, as we shall see.) The peculiar brand of Christianized paganism that formed the religion of the Russian masses before the revolution is felt in Yesenin's descriptions of nature, in his animistic epithets, in his quaint mysticism that often borders on sacrilege. There is no intentioned blasphemy in his reference to "bovine God," or in his shout: "Calve, O Lord!" for just as tenderly he addresses his Russia, the "sacred heifer," than whose "bovine eyes there are none better, there are no finer." His love for his native land, for its "pastoral sadness," its huts and songs, fields and groves, raspberry dawns and melancholy willows, has rustic freshness and color. His moon is "a curly lamb strolling through blue grass," or a colt harnessed to a sleigh, or a golden puppy. His sky has just calved and it "licks a red calfling," or again it "trembles, and out of the stall it leads a cloud by the bridle," or it may be an udder, and the stars its teats, while sunrise across the roof is a kitten washing its mouth with its paw.

Yesenin accepted the revolution with joy, and endeavored to attune himself to the new order, even unto tackling the "potbellied

Das Kapital." But the triumph of the city workers and the accelerated urbanization and mechanization of the country alarmed the Ryazan peasant, if only subconsciously. In his semimystic poems greeting the revolution Yesenin dreamed of a "peasant paradise," the realization of the ancient aspirations of all land tillers, that is, an unchangeably bucolic idyl of peace and plenty. The Bolshevik Revolution, on the other hand, meant to explode all proprietary dreams, including those of the village petty proprietors. The slow rustic tempo was to be quickened, to be changed by the machine, the "Iron Messiah" of the new proletarian poets. In Yesenin the "Iron Guest" provoked fear and sadness. He saw the passing of his "rye Russia" under the onslaught of metallic "America." There is pathetic nostalgia in his description of a red-maned colt galloping in the wake of a train that speeds "on its paws" across the steppe, and "snorts with iron nostrils": "The dear, dear funny fool! O where, where is he racing? Does he not know that steel cavalry has vanquished live horses?"

Yesenin shared this fear of the "Americanization" of Holy Russia with such other peasant-poets of his day as Oreshin (b. 1887), Klyuyev (b. 1887), Klychkov (b. 1889). Of these, Klyuyev was most uncompromising in his loyalty to the patriarchal village, steeped in pagano-Christian mythology and primitiveness of living conditions. Klyuyev's poetry remained to the end unadulterated in its peasant motives and form, reminiscent of old North Russian songs in rhythm, ornateness, and vocabulary. He bitterly reproached Yesenin for letting himself be contaminated by the city. It should be noted that these peasant-poets represented and expressed not the overwhelming mass of a pauperized peasantry, who had "nothing to lose but their chains," but the comparatively well-to-do small farmers, the actual or potential *kulaks*. Hence their nostalgia for the "idyllic" village.

Yesenin's "contamination" was unquestionable. His swift literary success, his popularity with the bohemia of Petrograd and

Moscow, his travel abroad with the exotic Isadora Duncan, made him replace his bast shoes and homespun blouse with patent-leather boots and swallowtails, literally and figuratively. But his urbanization was as incomplete and skin-deep as his attempted Marxianization. The asphalt pavements did not erase the mother soil from his memory. There were tears in his banter about raising his top hat when passing a cow painted over a butcher shop, or about his impulse to lift the tail of a cabman's mare and carry it "like the train of a duchess." "I am the last poet of the village," begins one of his lyrics of doom and despair.

In this mood were composed most of the verses of his "Barroom Moscow" cycle. Their nervous rhythm is reminiscent of gypsy romances, and also of Blok's late poems of mystic despondency. Yesenin is talking of himself and to himself, in drunken abandon, vainly trying to drown in liquor the heartache of a lost man, out of tune with the new environment, corroded by inner contradictions, and convinced of his hopelessness:

> Yes, 'tis definite now. Irrevocably
> I have forsaken my native fields.
> No longer with their winged foliage
> Will the poplars tinkle above me.
> With me away, the old house will hunch up.
> My old hound expired long ago.
> In Moscow's crooked streets
> God must have destined me to die.
> I love this embroidered city,
> However flabby, however senescent.
> Golden drowsy Asia
> Slumbering upon her cupolas.
> And at night, when the moon shines,
> When he shines . . . the devil, how he shines!
> I wend my way, head drooping,
> Through an alley, to a familiar bar.
> Noise and din in this dreary den,
> But all through the night, until dawn,

I read my verses to prostitutes,
And swill alcohol with bandits.
My heart beats quicker and quicker,
My speech grows incoherent.
"Like all of you, I am done for.
There's no comeback for me.
With me away, the old house will hunch up.
My old hound expired long ago.
In Moscow's crooked streets
God must have destined me to die."

Yesenin did make a last attempt to drag himself out of the mire.
He wrote a number of verses under the title "Soviet Russia,"
wherein he sounded a hymn to the new order, the new man and
his hopes and aspirations. His sincerity could not be questioned,
but it was patent that his ecstasy came from the head, not from
the heart. Indeed, the very change of conditions and their improvement made him feel the more keenly his loneliness, his being out
of place in the new environment. He exclaims:

What a country!
But then—what the devil!
Did I bellow in verse of being one with the people?
My poetry is no longer wanted here.
And very likely I myself am not wanted here.

The later Yesenin struck a congenial note among certain citizens. In those years of transition, when the heroics of revolution
and civil war were giving room to the practical heroism of reconstruction, that is, when military communism was replaced by the
NEP, there was no lack of bewilderment. Many a young man
found it irksome, after years of stormy battle and cosmic slogans,
to settle down to humdrum work in bureau or factory. When, in
1925, Yesenin shut himself in his hotel room in Leningrad, cut his
wrists and hanged himself, after leaving a dispirited farewell poem,
he provoked a sinister wave of sympathy and emulation. The soil
was ready for that mood of out-of-placeness and despair which

came to be called "Yeseninism." The need of combating this defeat-
ist state of mind was felt to be urgent among leading Bolsheviks.
We have noted Mayakovsky's immediate reaction to Yesenin's
suicide, and his "defection" five years later.

After the death of Yesenin the imagist group was hardly heard
of again. As a matter of fact, in his last years he was getting farther
and farther away from that group, and his connection with it was
becoming as dubious as that of Mayakovsky with the futurist
band. They both outlived their "schools" and buried them with
their own deaths. So tenuous became the allegiance of individual
survivors to their groups that an article by Shershenevich in 1928
bore the title, "Do the Imagists Exist?" He answered the question
in the negative, with the consoling chuckle that "if imagism is now
dead, futurism is safely buried."

The imagists, in spite of their obnoxious exaggerations and bad
manners, contributed their mite to Soviet poetry. The image was
given a higher place, was cultivated to grow more clear-cut, more
suggestive, and more closely congenial to the subject matter.

CONSTRUCTIVISTS

Another offspring of futurism to rebel against its parent was constructivism. In the West this term has been applied chiefly to
modern trends in architecture, especially to functionalist currents
(Frank Lloyd Wright, Corbusier, *et al.*) stressing the proper uti-
lization of material and technique. In Russia constructivism was
much in evidence during the early years of the revolution in painting and sculpture, architectural designs (hardly ever carried out),
and stage settings. As a literary term it was first used in 1922, and
the Literary Center of Constructivism (L.C.C.), formed in 1924,
made its hullabaloo existence felt till 1930, when it disbanded. The
small membership of the group—barely half a dozen at its peak—
contained enough talent to warrant recognition at the time and to
justify a brief discussion here.

The tenets of literary constructivism were expressed in a number of essays and declarations by members of the group, obscure in phraseology and often contradictory. One may attempt a reduction of these ideas to a few understandable principles, abstracted from scattered statements but largely based on the writings of the chief theoretician of the group, Kornely Zelinsky (b. 1896). Constructivism appears to be a reflection of contemporary technique in production, designed for greater speed, economy, and capacity. The "style of our epoch" is epitomized in the coined word "loadification" (*gruzofikatsia*), that is, "the increased load of functions per unit of material" ("Declaration" of L.C.C.) With the development of plan and organization in human society, each unit of power is expected to produce increasingly useful action (Zelinsky). In poetry the word—the power unit—must be "loadified" with meaning; the components of a composition are functionally subordinated to the theme. The Declaration employs such technical phrases in defining constructivism as "a system of the maximal exploitation of the theme," or "a system of mutual functional justification of all the component artistic elements." The four basic principles of constructivism, on which the Declaration and the individual theoreticians agree, may be summed up thus:

1. The *dominant* of meaning. The subject, the theme, decides the form and substance of the composition.

2. Economy of means. This simple phrase in an article by Zelinsky, in 1928, replaced the term "loadification" used four years earlier.

3. Localization, or local semantics: the theme dictates the choice of specific words for characterization and description.

4. Introduction of prose methods into poetry.

As we shall presently see, Selvinsky's poetry both illustrated and advocated these principles. The theorists of the group made a good deal of noise about its tenets, out of proportion to their application.

. The fondness for technological, constructive terms is betrayed by such titles of their writings as *Literary Gosplan* (the abridged name of the State Planning Commission), or *Biznes* (Business). Their eagerness for marching with the time, for close participation in "the organized onslaught of the working class," was the more pathetic since the constructivists were decidedly nonproletarian in expression, as well as by origin and education. Aware of the tragedy of the old intelligentsia who found themselves out of tune and touch with the new Russia, their spokesman, Zelinsky, tried to emphasize the congeniality of the constructivists with the Soviet regime:

Constructivism, presenting to literature (and above all to poetry, since the majority of the constructivists are poets) the same demands that are put forth by socialist construction in all domains of culture, expresses the cultural aspirations of the new Soviet intelligentsia, who seek to play a part (nearest to them in spirit) in this general construction. One may say that constructivism expresses the birth of a new Soviet intelligentsia, in its ideology and world outlook extremely different from the former Russian intelligentsia, whether god-seeking or nihilistic, whether Oblomov-like or Onegin-like, but always impotently idealistic.

As a theory, constructivism, with its vague terminology and exaggerated adulation of technique, failed to voice, or to appeal to, the new intelligentsia. When its loyalty to the regime was put in question by Party organs, the group found no spokesman to defend its position, and it melted away. Incidentally, Kornely Zelinsky has outgrown his infantile verbiage, and is today one of the most active critics and organizers of poetry groups and courses.

As for the poets of the group, Selvinsky alone deserved both the orchids and the brickbats as a constructivist. The others either possessed too puny and ephemeral talent to matter, or, like Inber and Bagritsky, their allegiance to the "school" was only nominal. Vera Inber (b. 1891) continues to write urbane verse in regular meter; her only allegedly constructivist tendency is a penchant for narrative. Both she and Bagritsky (who will be discussed separately) had lent their names to the "movement" out of personal friendship for Selvinsky, a fellow Odessite. In passing, one may note that in a literary sense Odessa has been to Leningrad and Moscow what Chicago has been to New York in the current century. Discounting the extravagant claims of some of its local patriots for regional peculiarities, one must admit that Odessa has produced a considerable number of original authors, among these most of the constructivists, and such writers as V. Katayev (b. 1897), I. Ilf (1897–1937) and Eugene Petrov (1903–1942), V. Shklovsky (b. 1893), Y. Olesha (b. 1899), V. Kaverin (b. 1902), S. Kirsanov (b. 1906), I. Babel (b. 1894), L. Slavin, and others. Group membership was often dictated by a vague *esprit de corps* among uprooted Odessites.

Selvinsky.—Ilya Selvinsky (b. 1899) may be regarded as a futurist of a later vintage, even though the principles of constructivism were in large part induced from his poetry and have remained, at bottom, his to this day. Constructivism presented a reaction against futurism, just as futurism had been a revolt against symbolism. Conversely, symbolism formed the starting point of futurism, and futurism served as a point of departure for constructivism. As previously observed, a new movement, whether in art or thought or politics, is almost invariably an heir to its predecessor, the fundamental traits of which it furthers, however much it may reshape and modify them. An absolute, topsy-turvy revolution is rare in history. Constructivism inherited the formalistic tendencies of futurism, but, born a decade later, it lent these tendencies a new, postrevolutionary aspect. Selvinsky's verse makes one recall Mayakovsky and other futurists by its novel rhythms, unusual vocabulary and rhymes, deliberate obscurity ("estrangement"), and other formal features. But Selvinsky came at a time when shocking iconoclasm and bombastic declarations were being replaced by constructive organizational work in all phases of life; this change was marked in his poetry. He differed at the outset both from the early futurists, preoccupied with form at the expense of content, and from their later variant, the LEF's, who advocated the reduction of literature to newspaper reportage and placard slogans. Selvinsky

demonstrated the constructivist principle of purposeful organization in poetry, the dominant subject matter organically unified
with its form. His compositions served as a model for "expediential
poetry," the term used in the sense of making the material fit perfectly the construction, by means of "localizing," specifying the
material (words and images) for each given subject. Selvinsky likewise furnished, in advance of the constructivist theory, the practical
illustration of rejecting "pure lyricism" in favor of the "inflation
of prose methods." This "inflation" meant the concretization of
poetic themes, their expansion and permeation with as much so-
ciality as was expected from the prose of the moment. Selvinsky's
poetry is seldom devoid of the narrative element; it is fondly interspersed with economic facts and figures, business items, docu-
mentary data, statistics: "Like any other poet, I am the heart of
statistics," he proclaims. In a note on "The Code of Constructivism" he wrote:

If we compare prose to a mirror and poetry to a brook, their likeness and
divergence becomes clear: prose, like a mirror, exists for the most part
teleologically, "in order to," whereas poetry, in the same way as a brook,
is primarily causal, "because of."

Hence the need of "mirrorizing the brook," of rendering poetry
more effective through the use of prose methods.

A minute analysis of constructivist principles practiced by Selvinsky is outside the scope of this essay; besides, his poetry is interesting enough to merit a less tedious approach. It has an unrivaled
power of conveying images with a precision that rouses in the
reader almost tactile sensations. Selvinsky achieves this both by
means of his constructivist method (precise fitness of construction
material) and because by nature he observes the world with an
inexhaustible avidity which goads him to visualize things fully
and exactly. This is true also of his auditory perception. In his early
"Gypsy Romances" and in the Cossack songs running through
Ulyalyayevshchina, he employs odd devices to make us hear the

exact diction of the Gypsies and the Cossacks. He doubles and
triples consonants, inserts additional vowels, places secondary ac-
cents, separates syllables by stop signs and question marks, and
even uses the letter "h," which does not exist in the Russian alphabet. The result is a typographical oddity, but in any case the reader
is enabled to get the nasal drawl and torrid exoticism of the Gypsy
songs, as well as the savage abandon and choral quality of Cossack
cavalry ditties.

Once in a great while Selvinsky forgets himself, as it were, and
creates atmosphere in the manner of "old" poetry, by such suggestive lines as these:

> Lilac clouds. Gray field.
> Appeasement and splendor.
> Piebald birches in golden pain.
> A pensive jade with a daw on its rump.

As a rule, he prefers concrete and precise details—Flemish *Klein-
malerei* in relief, if this were possible. He delights in describing
such ordinary scenes as the eating of *borshch* (beet soup) by the
bandit Dydla:

> Diving beneath the eye-full gold of the fluid,
> The wooden spoon with its peeled mouth
> Rocked the cabbage bulbs and membranes
> And the *borshch* swayed, fat and russet.

With the same eager care he watches, and makes us watch, the
murder of Ulyalyayev by his perfidious band:

> Dydla drew to his cheek the carbine.
> Tsok—missed fire. Then Pavlov the rifle
> Shoved into his mouth—and a golden gleam
> Lit the teeth from the inside.

> Out his nostrils purple blood and smoke.
> His face, as by lightning, twitched in pain.
> From his skull gushed with a gulping sound
> Gorgeous plumes of scarlet fluid.

Someone else pulled the carbine.
His fingers crooked, as though frozen numb.
Someone cravenly yelled: "Slash!"
Sabers crossed his nose and lips.

But one white eye looked on, unblinking.
Now the gullible took fright a bit:
Nothing seems to get the devil, nor sword nor bullet,
Though his mug is slashed in two, and the skull—just a hole.

To make sure of his death, the bandits resort to the "forefathers' execution": they chop off Ulyalyayev's head with an ax.

Selvinsky "inflates the prose methods" both in making nearly all his poems narrative and in unfolding his characters through dialogue. His long poems are novels or dramas in verse. *Ulyalya-yevshchina,* for example, deals with an imaginary band of brigands during the civil wars in the southeast of Russia, *Army Commander* 2 presents another civil war episode; *Pushtorg* is a picture of the NEP period; *Pao-Pao* is the story of an orang-outang turned human and almost Marxian; *Cheluskiana* is an epopee of Otto Schmidt's arctic expedition, and the heroic rescue of the "Cheluskin" crew by Soviet aviators; *Johann the Knight* is the tragedy of Ivan Bolotnikov, leader of a peasant revolt during the Troubled Times (early seventeenth century). In all these the development of the plot (often involved and obscure) is arrested by long discourses designed to build up the individual characters, and to express their, and the author's, views on a variety of questions. Thus, in *Ulyalyayevshchina,* amid descriptions of battles and banditry, he interpolates the intellectual Stein's incisive, often debatable, opinions on such subjects as the art of Cézanne in relation to Japanese technique, or François Villon and Edgar Allan Poe. He even manages to deal a pin-prick to Yesenin's imagism, by having Stein quote him:

"For example: 'Over blue Russia stands on guard
The old maple on one leg.'

> And where is the other? Quench my nerves,
> Or am I to wear armor against such legerdemain?
>
> Do you perceive the gracefulness of a tree
> Balancing on a *point,* ballerina-like?"

When asked how he would improve on Yesenin, Stein replies:

> "A master would say: 'The one-legged maple,'
> And at one stroke drive the image into its setting."

In *Pao-Pao,* Selvinsky has his characters discuss the capitalistic system and how it differs from the Soviet system. In conversational blank verse he surveys economic and social conditions throughout the world, at times hitting the nail on the head in sharp concise repartees. Thus, when Pao-Pao reproaches his workmen for being less zealous than the Russians, who "in storm and in cold beat world records," his men reply that "it is not the Russian workman who is good, but the Soviet workman. . . . There, work is not aimed at the masters' cashbox. . . . There, indeed, labor rules." Or, again, the immense wealth of modern society and its technical advancement bring Pao-Pao's observation:

> "Is there aught you haven't got? You have everything but happiness.
> Happiness—that's your only deficit item."

Not unlike *Ulyalyayevshchina, Pao-Pao* serves as a rostrum for the discussion of general topics, including literature and painting. Selvinsky's own views on art follow or alternate with pseudo-Marxian notions at one time in vogue among Soviet citizens. With concentrated irony he draws a scene in the Paul Gauguin room of a Moscow museum of modern art. A woman guide rattles on:

> We are now coming to Gauguin. Like
> Many and many others, Gauguin lived
> At the very height of the power concentration
> Of capitalistic society.
> And he, as a son of this society,
> Endeavored to serve its aims.

> For instance: here are Tahitians in nature's bosom,
> Little parrots here and there. Nice marine view.
> But do we see here the exploitation of colonies?
> No, that we do not see!

The guide typified the phase of "vulgarized Marxism" in Soviet
art and letters. After pointing at a bull on one of the canvases, and
impressing on her audience that out of the bull's hide were produced whips for the plantation slaves, the benighted young woman
rushes the comrades to the next room, where she is going to "in-
terpret" Cézanne. But Pao-Pao, the humanized orang-outang, de-
tains the workers and offers his reactions to Gauguin's paintings
of Tahiti:

> Strindberg wrote to Gauguin: *"Mon vieux,*
> You are putting my taste to dire trials:
> You show me plants no botanist knows about,
> Beasts Cuvier never heard of.
> These orange hounds,
> These tones, swashbuckling tones . . .
> Who are you, dear fellow? Frankly, I do not know.
> A savage who hates civilization?"
> Gauguin answers Strindberg: "Friend!
> The artist is only his model's pupil.
> The Maori gods have guided as they willed
> The docile valor of my hands.
> You see no invention, no embellishment:
> Here is a genuine epos of a small race!
> For all the academies of Kurfürstendamm
> I shall not exchange my barbarity."
> And right he was! A pupil of Pissarro,
> A checkplayer at dissolving colors,
> Here, at Tahiti, he plucked a plume
> From the tail
>   of the very
>   sun!
> Superb tones, sonorous, bell-like bass,
> Each stroke—a thousand tons.
> Look: this gold of women's bodies

> Resembles trees. The trees
> Look like women. All the ancient,
> All the magnetic force of nature
> Has poured into this peacock whirlwind,
>   Into this pagan ode!

Pao-Pao grows nostalgic in front of Gauguin's sophisticated primitives. In his enthusiasm for the South Sea paradise, one hears Selvinsky's own longing for "our prehistoric childhood." The workers in the end dismiss as pre-1917 stuff Pao-Pao's rhapsody of Gauguin's Tahiti:

> Labor for us is the realm of bending yoke,
> For them, only play of muscle and bone.
> Labor for us is the horse's bridle,
> Damned and accursed.
> Labor for them, a pleasant excuse
> For a trip to the mountain or ocean.
> That which seems to you a primitive
> Is the wisdom of bodies, the directive of genes!
> "My purpose," Gauguin used to say,
> "Is to sing the possibility of being happy."

Selvinsky has obvious faults, such as making his compositions topheavy with intellectual digressions, plot entanglements, an excess of naturalism in his gloating over tangible details, and occasional language oddities, "estrangement" features. He remains, however, a conspicuous figure in Soviet poetry, exuberant, eager, responsive to life and its problems, and decidedly maturing and shedding his early extravagances. In his latest long poem, *Johann the Knight* (1939), Selvinsky shows a growing earnestness and simplicity. His treatment of the Bolotnikov uprising is historically cautious, considering the meagerness of available data. Far from idealizing the revolting peasants, he displayes their ignorance and credulity, and their consequent victimization by rival factions of the nobles seeking personal gain during the Troubled Times. The tragedy of Bolotnikov, a peasant who happened to live abroad and taste of Western culture, and whose homesickness brought him back to lead the revolt, is the familiar tragedy of an individual ahead of his time. *Johann the Knight* is written in a colorful Russian, not overburdened with seventeenth-century archaisms, and free from "estrangement." Indicative of Selvinsky's evolution is the form of this poem: it is composed in blank iambic pentameter. In a statement made a few years ago Selvinsky justified his "tactometric" verse, with its irregularities and whimsical rhythms, as prompted by his "natural inclination." Regular meter repelled him as a feature of the hated past; specifically, iambics were "against his grain, with something of the glitter of epaulets in them." Now he is happily reverting to the Pushkin tradition.

BAGRITSKY

Eduard Bagritsky (1895–1934) was a member of the Constructivist Literary Center for some five years, but he bore no consistent allegiance to any school. His output, considerable for the short span of his life, is somewhat eclectic, showing traces of Robert Burns (a few of whose poems he lovingly translated) and other Western Europeans, as well as of a multitude of Russians, from Pushkin through the acmeists and futurists. Such traces, however, may be found in any well-read author, and it is futile to use them as a basis for any specific label. Bagritsky's verses vary in form, from regular meter (with a partiality for the amphibrach) to blank metric and free verse, futuristic broken lines, and arbitrary rhythms. As to subject, it ranges from Tyll Eulenspiegel and the romantic beggars of Burns to contemporary themes, the leading one being civil war episodes. His main work, on which his reputation stands, is *Elegy on Opanas,* a narrative poem, wherein epic mingles with ballad, and classic passages alternate with national motives from the ancient *Lay of Prince Igor* and from folk songs. The very name of the elegy, *Duma,* suggests Bagritsky's affinity with the celebrated Taras Shevchenko (1814–1861), author of numerous *dumy* (the name applied to Ukrainian folk epics and songs); the text reveals further signs of this kinship.

The poem is saturated with Ukrainian color, in both landscape and motives. Opanas is an Ukrainian peasant, unwittingly swept by the waves of revolution and civil wars into the camp of Makhno's "Greens," a variety of bandits midway between Reds and Whites, with anarchistic pretensions. Bagritsky conveys the gaudy romance of the strife by a variety of means, now by delicately suggestive images, now by Gargantuan revelry in gory detail. Woven into the large epic canvas is the personal drama of Opanas, the simpleton who was jolted out of his peaceful rusticity by a group of Bolshevik grain collectors led by the Jew Kogan. Resentful of the highhanded methods of the city chaps, Opanas joins the Makhno band, and is soon transformed into a picturesque brigand. His costume is an eloquent record of his exploits: a shaggy Cossack cap, a fur coat "taken off a dead rabbi near Gomel," a "French" military jacket of "English cut," stripped probably off some White officer, protégé of the Entente powers, lastly a revolver dangling from the chain of a church censer. Luck is with him, as his squad surprises at night Kogan and his company, and to Opanas falls the honor of executing the Bolshevik.

> Opanas moves back one leg,   "How do you do, comrade Kogan?
> He stands, he flaunts: Shave? You're next!"

An improbable note, perhaps admissible in an epic ballad, is introduced when Opanas, leading his captive to the wall, is revolted by the thought of killing an unarmed man, and offers to let Kogan escape. Not more probable is Kogan's refusal to be saved. To be sure, he reasons that his chance for escape from a Makhno camp is extremely slim, but what he says to Opanas sounds like grand opera:

> "Opanas, work clean,   'Tis unseemly for a communist
> Don't blink the aim.   To run like a wolfhound."

Bagritsky manages to avoid the impression of mock heroics, chiefly by means of colloquial dialogue. He likewise succeeds in suggesting the brooding mood of Opanas, after he shoots Kogan. Haunted by the image of the fearless Bolshevik, Opanas, captured by the Reds, confesses having executed Kogan, and pays with his life.

This skeleton of the poem can hardly give an approximate idea of its power and colorfulness. Bagritsky combines a gift for describing dramatic scenes, battles, surging crowds, executions, with the typical Ukrainian badinage that one finds in Gogol or Shevchenko. He tempers the pathos of fratricidal war and pitiless carnage by the contrasting tone of everydayness, by bits of homely colloquialism and banter, of folk song and folk wisdom. Above all, what makes Bagritsky dear to the Soviet reader is that in this *Elegy*, as in most of his poems, he is free from the allegedly Russian pessimism. Whatever the subject, even during the long torment of his dying days, Bagritsky expressed a passionate affirmation of life, an exuberant love for the sensuous, and an indestructible trust in man and mankind.

FORMALISTS

"Formalism" is a fitting term under which to sum up the account of nonrealistic tendencies treated in this chapter, since the word has been applied both to a general current in Russian literature, and other arts, of recent decades, and to a specific literary school. Taken in its broad meaning of preoccupation with form, formalism manifested itself in Russian art time and again, as a reaction against the predominance of social motives. In the twentieth century, triumphant symbolism, which had done much for the enrichment and refinement of Russian poetry (and, in a lesser measure, of Russian prose), engendered a number of further attempts in this direction, such as acmeism, futurism, imagism, constructivism. All these had in common the tendency of exclusiveness, of appeal-

ing to the few. After 1917, there was a general effort on the part
of leading poets of these schools to readjust themselves, to harness
their unusual and outlandish methods of expression to the service
of the new ruling element, the masses. We have noted the evolutionary steps of Mayakovsky and his comrades, from futurism to
LEF, thence to New LEF and REF. The same process took place
among the constructivists, notably Selvinsky. It may be said, in
sum, that for some two decades these poets have tried to live down
their formalistic penchants, or at least to subordinate them to social
motives.

Specifically, the term formalists was applied to a group of theorists who, starting in 1916, became especially active during the 1920's
in subjecting the study of literature and its history to a laboratory
method. This approach was new in Russia, where save for a few
essays by symbolists the sociological method had predominated.
There resulted a number of refreshing and scholarly studies of
poetics and style, and of such individual authors as Pushkin, Gogol,
Nekrasov, Dostoyevsky, Tolstoy. Along with their analysis of
earlier literature, many of the formalists undertook to direct contemporary writers, and it is here that they proved both divergent
and controversial.

Without attempting to discuss the intriguing varieties of formalism, I shall limit myself to the basic ideas of its leading
spokesmen. These all agree that art has a value in itself and is not
dependent on life and its problems. "Art has always been free from
life, and its color never reflected the color of the flag that waved
over the city's fortress" (Shklovsky). The nonpolitical attitude was
avowed by such formalistic writers as the "Serapion Brothers." But
that was not all. Art must be free not only from politics, but also
from philosophy and psychology (which would imply a complete
departure from the models set up by Dostoyevsky and Tolstoy).
"To impute to a poet ideas and feelings is just as absurd as the be-
havior of medieval audiences that beat up the actor who played the

part of Judas" (Yakobson). Shklovsky, the most clever, versatile, and influential member of the group, defines literary productions as "the weaving of sounds, articulative motions, and thoughts," but he goes on to delimit thought in a literary work either as "a foreign body" or as auxiliary "material, like the pronunciatory and sonant features in a linguistic morpheme."

In the formalistic theory words acquire a self-sufficient value, as material does for the builder. The material, we are told, is for the artist not merely a means, just as stone is more than a means for the sculptor, but is a "lump of existence, a lump of the concrete truth which he is impelled to discover." In the same way verbal aesthetics sublimates the word beyond its everyday insignificance:

The word is a definite material which in everyday life serves only as a means, as does stone, paint, sound, or motion. Transferred from the practical to the aesthetic field, it [the word] unfolds all its hidden life that has accumulated for ages. (Eikhenbaum, b. 1886.)

There is an obvious contradiction between the treatment of the word as a self-sufficient entity and giving it an "unfolding" purpose. But then, contradictions are inevitable in a raw theory, and the formalists are fearless enough to dismiss contradictions as irrelevancies. Shklovsky himself, the advocate of words *an und für sich,* free of sense and ideas, assigns to the word an important functional role. In his *Theory of Prose* he discusses the "automatization" of our movements, actions, and sensations, by dint of habituation and endless repetition. The sensation of holding a pen in your hand for the first time is quite lost when you pick up the pen for the ten-thousandth time. Thus, objects and concepts wither away:

Automatization devours objects, clothes, furniture, your wife, your fear of war. Now in order to render a stone stony, there exists what is called art. The purpose of art is to convey the sensation of an object as visualization, not as cognition. The device of art is "estrangement" (*ostraneniye*) of things and difficult form, which increases the difficulty of receptivity and its duration: the receptual process in art is a self-aim, and should be prolonged. "Art is a method of living through the process of making a thing, whereas that which is accomplished in art is unimportant!"

This emphasis on difficult and "estranging" form naturally leads the formalists to champion all exclusive schools of literature, from misty symbolism to word-distorting futurism and its derivatives. In prose they hail the replacement of the psychological novel of Tolstoy and Dostoyevsky by "forms of complex subject matter," by novels of adventure (Eikhenbaum). Shklovsky regards Sterne's *Tristram Shandy* as "the most typical novel of world literature," and Sterne as "an extreme revolutionary of form." He delights in Sterne's method of "laying bare his device," of playing with form in an arbitrary fashion, bewildering the reader with unexpected deviations and digressions on noses, fortifications, and what not, with unmotivated backward and forward leaps in the course of the narrative. The discursive charm of Sterne's style is evident in most of Shklovsky's own writings, obviously in his record of the revolutionary days, entitled *A Sentimental Journey:* he lightly mingles facts with fiction, critical essays with personal reminiscences, earnest theorizing with anecdotical banter. Anecdotism became a leading feature in formalist fiction, notably in Shklovsky's precious trifles, in Kaverin's fantastic grotesques wherein he out-Hoffmanns Hoffmann, even in Tynyanov's (b. 1894) historical novels and novelettes. These authors deliberately avoid deep analysis, the traditional Russian introspection, flaunting instead a mass of external detail arranged in a complex pattern, with emphasized "estrangement." In passing, it should be noted that these and other writers of that group have gradually discarded their mannerisms, and have produced in recent years distinguished fiction, no longer free from social motives, and almost free from anecdotal and ornamental extravagances. Kaverin's *Fulfillment of Desires,* and Tynyanov's unfinished *Pushkin* may serve as illustrations.

It is rather curious that so keen a literary commentator of the sociological camp as L. Trotsky (1870–1940) should credit the formalists with having "raised the theory of art, and partly art itself, from the state of alchemy to the position of chemistry." The valuable contributions of certain formalists to literary criticism, theory, and history, cannot be gainsaid; they have helped to free the subject from irrelevant excrescences and stifling narrowness. Shklovsky, Tynyanov, Eikhenbaum, and, even more, such academically trained scholars as Tomashevsky (b. 1890) and Zhirmunsky (b. 1891) have laid the foundations for a healthy, unbiased study of literary problems. This is true of most of their essays on specific subjects and on individual authors.[8] But the extreme generalizations of those who assumed the role of high priests of formalism have an air of charlatanism. One wonders how Trotsky was misled by the allegedly scientific verbiage of their formulas, such as the notorious theorem of Shklovsky: "The content of a literary composition equals the sum of its stylistic devices." This oft-quoted maxim, along with other tenets of formalism I have briefly touched upon, would reduce literature, and art in general, to a mechanical craft in which methods, devices, predominate and push to the background, if they do not eliminate, ideas, emotions, social issues.

Paradoxically enough, formalism, which at first glance is nothing if not a plea for the divorce of art from life and reality, became coupled with a seemingly opposite tendency, branded as naturalism by the adherents of socialist realism. Though scornful of content, as something unimportant and at best subordinate in art, the formalists, at least their more conspicuous leaders, sang in unison with the later variant of futurism, LEF. "Literature of fact," or, to use their hybrid word, "factography," was vociferously demanded by leading LEFists like Brik (b. 1888), Chuzhak (b. 1876), Tretyakov (b. 1892), and . . . Shklovsky! They declared themselves

---

[8] In his acute studies of nineteenth-century Russian writers, Eikhenbaum occasionally allowed his formalism to drive him to extremes. Thus he reduced Gogol's prose and Nekrasov's verse to a problem of style, of verbal innovations, the subject being only a "pose," a motivation of the formal composition. He was less extravagant in his essays on Tolstoy.

opposed to fiction, to invention, to imitation of life: all that was "opium for the people." Soviet literature must be actual, factual, must be a part of constructive life. The height of literary expression in an age of seething activity is reportage, is the newspaper. "What the Bible was for the medieval Christian—a guide for every occasion in life—what the novel with a message was for Russia's liberal intelligentsia, that the newspaper of our day is for the Soviet activist" (Tretyakov). What LEF preached and practiced rather ineffectually, was indirectly followed by certain groping writers who loaded their descriptions with an excessive abundance of detail, thus hoping to reproduce reality. The years of war and revolution were so rich in adventure and extraordinary events that contemporary writers felt incapable of coping with life as a whole, and compromised by turning their lens on one limited corner of the land during one particular fraction of the period, and described that "fully." Such was most of the prose and of narrative poetry during the first years after the revolution—episodic, locally colorful, factual, stark. It appeared to be a literature of facts, not of life. Through the multitude of details one failed to see life itself in its complexity. These "naturalistic" authors ultimately proved to be as far removed from actual life as the formalists who frankly divorced themselves from it.

It is noteworthy that formalism, of whatever shades and variations, held its ground for some twenty years after the revolution. It was manifest in all the arts and, of course, in aesthetics and criticism. That so exclusive and precious a tendency was tolerated under a regime taken to be an expression of the tastes and standards of the masses, showed to what an extent these tastes were still guided and influenced by the nonproletarian intelligentsia. With the growing consciousness of the masses, and with the increased number and strength of their own intelligentsia, the common attitude toward formalistic features became more and more adverse. At the same time, Marxian critics waged a systematic war against what they regarded as the residue of bourgeois decadence. The formalists were compelled to be on the defensive. Some of them disavowed their formalism; Zhirmunsky, for example. Others sought a compromise in suggesting a hybrid formal-sociological school, in which Marxians would investigate the content, and formalists the form of literature. Finally the impatience with formalistic poetry, music, drama, and other arts became so general that the ruling Party felt constrained to take a hand in the matter.

In 1936, the Party organ, *Pravda* ("Truth"), launched a campaign against formalistic tendencies in art. The immediate provocation was caused by the performance of young Shostakovich's (b. 1906) opera *Katerina Izmaylovna,* based on Leskov's (1831–1895) story, *Lady Macbeth of the Mtsensk District.* The *Pravda* editorial condemned the opera as a deliberate distortion of symphonic sounds, which made it inaccessible to the ears of the masses. The article aroused a general discussion, in the press and at public meetings, of similar trends in other arts, including the stage and literature. Public opinion demanded a return to healthy realism and understandability. Shostakovich in music, Meierhold in the theater, and other formalists, were given a resolute reprimand by their audiences.

Foreign observers interpreted this organized attack against formalism as another instance of dictatorial tyranny. Critics lamented the official clamps imposed upon the gifted Shostakovich, and were even more outraged by the dismissal of Meierhold, the veteran director and daring innovator, whose activity began with the opening of the Moscow Art Theater, in 1898, and went through numerous phases and changes, culminating in a series of bold experiments after the October revolution. There is no denying the fact that such measures restrict the freedom of the artist to create as he sees fit. Soviet audiences have grown in numbers and in influence; they have acquired immense power, and have exercised this power to demand that the artist subordinate his personal whims and idio-

syncrasies to an earnest and true evaluation of life and its reflection
in an understandable way. It is not ungratifying to record that
such censure does not necessarily discourage talent and produc-
tivity. Shostakovich, for example, has since produced his universally acclaimed Fifth, Sixth, and Seventh symphonies and other
robust compositions that lead one to believe in the helpfulness of
serious public criticism. Meierhold, once more given the opportu-
nity to direct, admitted his formalistic vagaries in a speech before
an all-Union conference of stage directors (1939). A few passages
from his speech are worth citing:

> We must bring to light the fundamental mistakes of the formalists and
> naturalists, so that these mistakes may not be repeated. We who had erred,
> who had caused considerable damage to art—myself, Shostakovich, and
> Sergey Eisenstein [b. 1898]—have been given full opportunities to work,
> and to rectify our mistakes.

One of these mistakes Meierhold considers to have been "the
substitution of external form for the inner content." He refers
specifically to his productions of Gogol's *Inspector General* and
Ostrovsky's *Forest,* and to Akimov's staging of Shakespeare's
Hamlet,[9] and concludes:

> Who knows what outrages the formalists might have committed in
> art, had they not been stopped in time. For this reason the closing of the
> theater which I had directed was perfectly just. This is a lesson for all
> those who follow wrong paths in art.

The extremes of formalism have gone the way of other extremes

---

[9] The liberties these directors took with classic and modern plays caused much
resentment and chagrin. Meierhold did not scruple about tampering with the text,
to suit his stage innovations, such as shifting panels and elevated planes. Akimov's
Hamlet acted as an unemployed prince who tried desperately to get the job of a
king, and went to the length of disguising himself as the ghost of his father, to
frighten his stepfather. Made up as a robust Holbein chap, Hamlet delivered "To
be or not to be" with a tankard of ale in one hand, as he leaned against the counter
of a taproom and addressed his audience—the bartender. Ophelia, jilted by Hamlet,
took to drink, and drowned while inebriated. Soviet audiences did not relish such
frivolities.

in life and art that were driven out of existence by the robust sense of the average Soviet citizen. Socialist realism militates against all narrow conceptions of art, both as to form and content. It embraces life in its visible and implied realities, beyond the surface of form and fact. It demands of the artist a vision, an ability to observe the present not as an isolated episode but as a link in the evolutionary chain of the history of mankind.

Chapter V ✧ Proletarian Poets and Theorists

Before 1917

THE WRITERS and groups thus far discussed belonged to what the Russians designate as the intelligentsia, in contrast to the common and uneducated folk. In a land of prevailing illiteracy, where education was the privilege of a well-to-do minority, the intelligentsia, especially those of creative ability, bore perforce the air of exclusiveness. The handful of commoners who broke through the heavy crust of disabilities and rose to the heights of administrative, intellectual, or artistic endeavor, automatically lost their allegiance to the common people, and swelled the ranks of the privileged. One might cite as examples Lomonosov (1711–1765) and Speransky (1772–1839). Even Gorky, who went on championing the unprivileged after emerging to the top, inevitably wrote for the intelligentsia, the only available audience. The same exclusiveness, if not in greater measure, obtained among the poets. Once in print and in literary form, such authentic peasant verses as those of Koltsov (1809–1842) and Nikitin (1824–1861), in the nineteenth century, were shut off from the illiterate masses, and were read by a tiny minority. The later poets, such as Klyuyev and Yesenin, further "sublimated" their poetic expression of folk motifs. It is patent that the writer cannot help addressing himself to his reader.

Russia's industrial proletariat was so small in numbers and so enslaved economically that it could hardly be expected to produce any artists. The handful of poems by factory workers that appeared during the last two decades of the nineteenth century made no impression save as freaks. Only in the present century did the rapidly awakening working class begin to emit a thin small voice in letters. Maxim Gorky, himself a "freak" in the lofty halls of the intelligentsia, had a great deal to do with the encouragement of proletarian talent. He tirelessly solicited and fostered manuscripts by "self-taught" (*samouchki*) writers, and from time to time acquainted the public with his findings. While at Capri, he organized at his villa a school for Russian workers, who were chosen for their intelligence and secretly sent abroad to prepare for leadership. Aside from political and economic subjects, these students were given literary instruction, Gorky himself being one of the lecturers. In 1914, Gorky edited the first anthology of proletarian writers, thirty-odd in number, some of whom grew to prominence after 1917 (e.g., Gastev [b. 1882], Gerasimov [b. 1889], Fillipchenko [b. 1887], Samobytnik-Mashirov [b. 1884], Pomorsky [b. 1891]). In his introduction to this anthology, addressed to the workers, Gorky wrote with encouraging confidence, and not without a note of prophecy:

122859

This book, written by your comrades, is a new and very significant event in your life. It speaks eloquently for the growth of intellectual forces amidst the proletariat. You understand, of course, that for a self-taught writer it is immeasurably harder to write a brief story than it is for a professional author to compose a long novel... and you understand that, aside from the lack of leisure, the worker-writer is prevented from expressing his ideas brilliantly and precisely, that is, artistically, by his limited ability to use the pen, the writer's tool, by his unfamiliarity with the technique of the craft, and above all by lack of words, by his inability to select from a dozen words or so the most simple and adequate. Yet, despite all these difficulties, I think that you may honestly say that this collection of yours is interesting, that you have reason to rejoice, and that—who can tell?—this small book may be mentioned in the future as one of the first steps of the Russian proletariat toward the creation of its own belles-lettres. "A fantasy," I shall be told: "There has been no such a literature ever or anywhere." We have many things today that formerly did not exist; certainly there has been no working class of such aspects and such spiritual content as we have today. I am simply convinced that the proletariat can create its own belles-lettres....

The anthology was impressive, indeed, both for the quality and the quantity of the hitherto unheard-of workers' talent (seventy out of the four hundred and fifty manuscripts submitted were accepted). Most of the poetry and prose dealt with the bitter lot of the workers, their barbarous living conditions, and their persecution by the authorities. Aside from this Jeremianic tone, there was also a new note of resolution and faith in the future. A goodly portion of the lyrics and stories were composed during such enforced leisure as prison or exile, merited by the author's participation in the revolutionary struggle. This glamour of martyrdom was apt to disarm too severe criticism of the collection, the stylistic qualities of which were rather pedestrian. The intelligentsia traditionally talked down, and charitably, to such extraordinary rarities. Opposition to being treated gently, as "freaks," began to appear among the workers themselves. Thus I. N. Kubikov (b. 1887), a self-made literary critic risen from the workers, warned against being carried away by illusions and "regarding baby babble in the field of art as the beginning of maturity." "Personally," he adds, "I think, and not only think but feel in my own case, that at a certain stage of his developing consciousness the advanced worker cannot be reconciled to being treated with a special yardstick, when for him, as a worker, they lower the requirements imposed on a proletarian writer by world history." This was written in 1914,[1] when it might have seemed precipitant to speak of such "requirements" from the worker as an artist. What the Russian worker had thus far achieved, in letters, was not much more than an inferior imitation of the bourgeois counterpart, even though the subject matter had novelty and pathos. How could one dream of a workers' art at a time when the average working day was eleven hours long, and the only free time the worker had was at night, after an exhausting day, or on his sickbed, or when in jail or in exile?

[1] *Nasha Zarya* ("Our Dawn"), No. 3.

THE OCTOBER REVOLUTION

Then came 1917. October[2] gave the workers responsibility and hegemony, in the form of proletarian dictatorship. The impossible, the illogical, and, from the point of view of the majority of western Marxians, the "unscientific" phenomenon became a reality: the most backward, least industrialized and proletarianized of the great countries proved to be the first to overthrow the system of private capitalism, and to make "a leap from the kingdom of necessity into the realm of freedom." One can hardly overestimate the sense of importance aroused in the workmen by the easy victory they gained, with the aid of the army, over bewildered and demoralized proprietary Russia. Yesterday pariahs, the workers suddenly rose to the heights of an aristocracy, a privileged class, leader, master, and ruler. Nothing seemed beyond the ken and power of the victorious proletariat, and if it could make and unmake values, destroy ancient institutions and relationships and replace them by new ones, if it could, in short, control social, political, and economic intercourse, what might not be its effect on culture in general, and art in particular?

This became a central question, which for fifteen years provoked a variety of answers and solutions, a multitude of disputes and discussions, collisions and battles with alternating victories and defeats for the numerous combatants. As in any war, there was waste of energy, avoidable passion and destruction, roughness and intolerance. At the same time, the long and bitter controversy cleared the air, demonstrated the erroneousness of many staunchly upheld notions, exploded a host of sacrosanct slogans, and helped to sober a number of hotheads and inflated imaginations. It would fill a volume to reproduce all the variants, zigzags, and shades of this war; only its highlights need be mentioned here.

---

[2] The Bolshevik Revolution took place on October 25, 1917, Old Style. By the Western calendar, now in force in Soviet Russia, the date was November 7. "October" has remained in use in a variety of derivatives symbolical of that revolution.

There were extremists on either side of the question whether, and how far, the dictatorship of the proletariat should extend over cultural values. One is, naturally, first impressed by the vehement demands of the newcomers, considering that only a handful of workers had been articulate, in letters, on the eve of the revolution. In poetry, and also in prose declarations, the triumphant class voiced its will to power, without compromise with the hateful past. Vladimir Kirillov's (b. 1889) "We" gave expression to this sentiment less raucously than a number of more aggressive effusions:

> We, innumerable dread legions of labor,
> We have conquered spaces of sea, ocean, and land.
> We have kindled cities with the light of artificial suns.
> Our proud souls burn with the conflagration of revolts.
> We are gripped by mutinous, passionate intoxication.
> Let them shout at us: "You are executioners of beauty!"
> In the name of our Tomorrow we shall burn Raphael,
> Shall demolish museums, trample on flowers of art.
> We have thrown off the load of oppressive heritage,
> We have rejected the chimeras of wisdom bled white—
> Our girls in the radiant kingdom of the future
> Shall be more beautiful than the Venus of Milo.
> Our eyes are drained by tears, our tenderness killed.
> We have forgotten the odor of grass and blossoms of spring.
> We have fallen in love with the might of steam and power of
>   dynamite,
> With the song of the siren, the motion of shafts and wheels.
> We have become kindred with metal, have merged our souls with
>   machines,
> We have unlearned to sigh and pine for heaven.
> We want everyone on earth to have enough to eat,
> No groans and wails for bread shall be heard.
>
> You poet-aesthetes, go on cursing Great Ham,
> Kiss the fragments of the past beneath our heels,
> Water with your tears the ruins of the broken temple:
> We are free, we are bold, we breathe a different beauty.

The muscles of our arms thirst for gigantic labor,
Our collective breast burns with a creative pang.
With marvelous honey we shall fill the comb to its brim.
We will find a new and dazzling road for our planet.

We love life, its intoxicating furious rapture.
Our spirit has been toughened by stormy struggle, by suffering.
We are everybody. We are in everything. We are a light-dimming
flame,
We are our own Deity and Judge and Law.

The omnipotent collective "We," obliterating the past, wedded to metal and the machine, determined to blaze a new path for our planet—that was the characteristic attitude of the new spokesmen for the working masses. To be sure, the rank and file neither felt nor spoke in Kirillov's manner, reminiscent of such "fragments of the past" as Verhaeren, Marinetti, and the mellifluous Balmont. The worker-poets chanted grandiloquently, with utter confidence in themselves and in their mission. Thus Ilya Sadofyev (b. 1889) summons the universe to meet the proletarians properly, arrayed in a crimson garb:

Like a bride awaiting the bridegroom's kisses,
Aflame with ecstasy, with languor,
Be ready for the tryst.
The forerunners of future ages are marching—
Proletarian writers, poet-bards,
They are sent by masses, throngs, millions,
Billions ...
Legions ..
... Sent as forerunners to dynamite the rocks of the past,
And prepare a path, fiery, clean, bright,
For the poet of the future.

Nor does Sadofyev refrain from glorifying the collective "We," in addressing his fellow poets:

We are messengers of the future new beauty.
We are the gait, we are the breath of new, fair aeons.
We are the heart, the brain of toilers, their finest flowers.

We are the world unity of labor's imperious aspirations.
We are the first to come forth and are first to march boldly
In serried close ranks, to the summons of new times.

PROLETCULT

Kirillov, Sadofyev, and other young poets who had recently
emerged from the mass of factory workers, filled the air of the
newborn state with their notes of joyous pride and boundless am-
bition. Their sentiment was not confined to the printed page, nor
to a score of dreamy poets. It spread among organized labor, and
found an ever-growing mass of adherents, under the banner of Proletarian Culture. At first in Petrograd and Moscow, then in other
centers, proletcult groups were organized, proletcult periodicals
began to appear, and as early as April, 1918, the government felt
impelled to open at the Commissariat of Public Education a "section of independent cultural-educational organizations—'Proletcult.' " While there was a variance of opinion in the editorials and
resolutions of these motley organs, they voiced a pretty common
conviction as to the mission of the proletariat to assume control of
the nation's culture. The first issue of *Gryadushcheye* ("Days to
Come") expressed this view in such editorial remarks as these:

> Bourgeois culture is decomposing like a corpse. . . . The great artist—the
> proletariat—is creating a new culture. . . . Let the bourgeois culture, based
> on slavery, property, and robbery, meet wrathfully the advent of the Great
> Artist. We shall close our ranks closer and firmer, we shall enthusiastically
> foster and gather all the flowers of proletarian creative effort.

The style and the images betray the "bourgeois" source of this
arch-proletarian statement. While some proletcult units and publications allowed for a "critical acceptance" of the culture of the
past, the prevailing sentiment was for a complete divorce. One of
the few (there were fewer than half a dozen at the time) proletarian writers of prose, Bessalko, advocated the total rejection of
former literature. "To those," he wrote, "who are worried because

proletarian writers do not try to fill the gap between old and new art, we say: So much the better! We are in no need of the link of continuity." The resolution of the Petrograd proletcult declared proletarian culture to be "all human," therefore entitled to "exclusive domination," and called upon the workers to fight for the organization of a "center of proletarian culture" that should direct "the whole business of national enlightenment and education." That meant the eventual abolition of the Commissariat of Education, whose head, Lunacharsky, was apparently not fully trusted. The proletarians displayed a snobbishness that savored of *nouveaux riches*. Thus, Valerian Lebedev-Polyansky (b. 1881) defined the working class as "a leader in the creation of a new culture," relegating the intelligentsia to the role of "experts, functionaries, machines, in part a material that has to be worked over—and that's all." At the all-Russian conference of proletarian writers, which was held at that early stage, a discussion developed about the attitude of their union toward writers from the intelligentsia and peasantry. The unanimously accepted resolution limited the membership to writers "who have come out of the workers' *milieu*, and who uphold the class point of view."

Within less than one year after the Bolshevik victory, the proletcult movement had become nation-wide and influential, with a "Central Committee of the All-Russian Council of Proletcult," and an official organ, *Proletarskaya kultura*. In September, 1918, the first all-Russian congress of "proletarian cultural-educational organizations" was held in Moscow. The speeches and discussions revealed a wide divergence of views. Class intransigence was demanded by the Petrograd proletcult, which instructed its delegates "to made no compromise whatever with bourgeois ideology." Its delegate, Samobytnik-Mashirov, a worker-poet, struck the keynote of the extremists at the congress:

Comrades, I greet you in the name of Red Petrograd. I am addressing you at a moment when the broadest perspectives are opening before us.

Everything is in the hands of the proletariat. Now is the time to talk about proletarian culture. There shall be not only words but deeds. It is true that we face a task of enormous responsibility, but it is my belief that we shall create new values. I wish I could find bright and powerful images to convey all the vitality and force of proletarian culture. *We must not yield to compromises.* Firmly and immutably holding to the class point of view, we shall proceed to create our own culture.

The opposite extreme faction tried to limit the functions of the proletariat to political and economic problems, confining their cultural activity to an effort at mastering the heritage. The historian M. Pokrovsky (1868–1932), Associate Commissar of Education, somewhat timidly expressed this view:

Enormous is the task lying before you, that of creating a proletarian culture. Perhaps I am an "old believer" in this case, and should be driven out of your midst, but I do think that the first step in the creation of a proletarian culture must be the complete assimilation of the culture already in existence, at least in its technical part. Let me remind you of him whose portrait adorns this hall—Karl Marx. Before writing *Das Kapital,* Marx had made a most thorough study of the old political economy, which merited such treatment, and only by standing on the shoulders of that literature was he able to rise to his position.

Between the notion of discarding all the old culture, and its extreme opposite, that of passively absorbing it before attempting to create a new one, there lay a variety of more moderate shades of opinion, from the "rightist" hues of Lunacharsky and Krupskaya (Lenin's wife), to the "leftist" of Bogdanov and Polyansky. After prolonged and heated debates, the congress adopted unanimously (one member not voting) the resolution offered by Bogdanov. Since the theses of the latter, with some variations, remained fundamental and binding for the "leftist" champions of proletarian culture, practically until 1932, they must be summarized here.

Bogdanov's Tenets.—One of the leaders in Gorky's school at Capri, A. Bogdanov (1873–1928), had been long preoccupied with the idea of proletarian culture. Bogdanov was one of the most learned men in the revolutionary intelligentsia, but the very breath of his erudition brought him at times dangerously close to dilettantism. A many-sided scientist, he was subject also to a certain mysticism, and while seeking concrete and demonstable knowledge,[3] he was capable of verbal generalizations devoid of a realistic basis. Lenin had serious disagreements with Bogdanov before the war, and in a number of letters conveyed his misgivings about "Bogdanovism" to Gorky (without immediate effect on Gorky, however). In the formative stage of the Soviet order, with Lenin and other leaders engaged in multitudinous and arduous tasks, Bogdanov slipped into the role of the high priest of proletcult, lending form and substance to the mass of dreams and vague notions that hovered in the feverish air of the time.

In the theses of his resolution, and in his numerous articles before the revolution and thereafter, in the central organ of proletcult, Bogdanov endeavored to work out a broad theory. He emphasized the importance of art as "the most powerful weapon for the organization of collective forces, and in a class society of class forces," since, by means of "living images," art organizes "social experience not only in the sphere of cognition but also in the sphere of feelings and aspirations." Heretofore the proletariat has carried on its struggle in politics and economics. Its weakness in the third aspect of the struggle, the cultural, explains the confusion of the working class during the World War, their inability to understand and defend their position, and their resultant submission to the leadership of the bourgeoisie. Complete class liberation depends on cultural liberation. The proletariat must take full possession of all available knowledge, of science, technology, and above all, of art, which is both a "broader" and "more powerful" instrument than science for the organization of the masses, because these find "the language of living images closer and more understandable."

---

[3] Bogdanov eventually perished in his laboratory, the victim of one of his fantastic experiments in blood transfusion.

Proletarian culture, says Bogdanov, differs in spirit from preceding cultures in that it is collectivist, and not authoritarian (as religious-feudal culture) or individualistic (as bourgeois culture). The principle of comradely coöperation is to guide the proletariat in taking over and readapting all the previous endeavors of the human mind. The role of the working class is to "organize the whole life of mankind fully and harmoniously." Here Bogdanov introduces a pet idea he had been working on for years, that of "universal organizing knowledge," which he regards as the main task of the proletcult and of his other brain child, the proletarian university. As an important part of this task Bogdanov advocates the cultivation of proletarian art, literature in particular, "to educate men in the spirit of profound solidarity, comradely coöperation, close brotherhood of fighters and builders welded by a common ideal."

Since he assigns to art the role of "organizing social experience" and man's "feelings and moods," Bogdanov makes the acceptability of art by the proletariat broad enough to include masterpieces of the past and present, even when their authors do not represent the proletarian point of view. The dilettante in Bogdanov makes him uncertain at this juncture. He accepts, for example, the value of antique sculpture, or of lyrical poetry, as long as they are good art, for then they inevitably evoke a social response. In such cases nothing is left of his prerequisite of "collectivism" as the only point of view on which proletarian art, and culture in general, must be based. Bogdanov's aesthetics is lacking in precision; when evaluating a work of art, he is often forced to employ decidedly un-Marxian terms. The Venus of Milo, religious paintings, folk tales and other nonproletarian productions Bogdanov endorses for their "beauty," for their ennobling and purifying quality, for the "expressiveness" with which they "transport you into another world and make you cognizant of that world as no scholarly presentation could." The materialistic class approach gives way to an idealistic classless attitude. Bogdanov goes so far as to deplore the publication of workers' verses, for the poor technique of which their revolutionary and proletarian sentiment cannot atone. Such laxity on the part of the editor and publisher he brands as "criminal." Proletarian critics must demand "complete accord between form and content," a formula which Bogdanov neglects to make clear and specific. "Art technique" must be learned by the proletarian artist from his predecessors, says Bogdanov. This brings us to the most heatedly debated question: How are the proletarians to treat their "predecessors" and the artistic heritage of the past? In his resolution, adopted by the congress, Bogdanov implied the acceptance of this heritage as taken for granted, though with reservations:

The treasures of old art must not be accepted passively, or they will bring up the working class in the spirit of the culture of the ruling classes and thus in the spirit of subjection to an order of life created by these classes. The proletarian must take the treasures of old art in the light of his critique, of his new interpretation, which discloses their hidden collectivist foundations and their organizational meaning. Then will these treasures prove a precious heritage for the proletarian, a weapon in his struggle against that same old world which had created them, and a weapon in the construction of a new world. The task of transmitting this artistic heritage lies on the shoulders of proletarian critics.

Proletcult in Practice.—Such are the basic principles of proletcult as voiced by its champion. In attempting to apply them, the leaders of the movement had to face further clashes—with one another and with outside forces. The resolution of the congress, which embodied Bogdanov's theses, was presently coupled with another one, adopted after a report read by the chairman-elect of the central committee, V. Lebedev-Polyansky. This resolution expressed the aims and methods of the organization more clearly and outspokenly. First of all, it demanded the autonomy of proletcult activities in the republic. This point was formulated a few months later in a clear-cut triad: "Proletcult is a creative cultural class organization of the proletariat, just as the workers' Party is its political, and the trade unions its economic organization." The resolution further demanded the full support of local and central state institutions. Based on collective labor and comradely coöperation, the organization aimed to "form a proletarian culture which, upon the abolition of class distinctions, shall become all-human." One of the means for the attainment of this aim should be the adoption of such achievements of the preceding culture as "bear an all-human stamp," these to be taken "critically, and to be worked over in the crucible of class-consciousness." For the purpose of creating its own literature, "basically distinct from the hitherto bourgeois literature," the proletcult was to encourage and "advance" its own writers, to unfold a publishing activity, and to open "literary studios" for the training of workers in the history of literature, its theory and practice.

The last-mentioned step seemed the most immediately practical method of preparing an army for the storming of the citadel of literature. To be sure, it was soon "discovered" that artists of the word cannot be produced in the mass by hothouse methods. But in any event, the "litstudios" were the one indisputably positive undertaking of the proletcult, since they answered a dire need for elementary education in matters of literature and of general culture. During the first three years of its existence the proletcult spread through the vast land, its branches sprouting not only in industrial centers, but in numerous backwood towns where the presence of proletarians was exceedingly doubtful. Contrary to its program and declarations, the proletcult, which was intended to be an exclusively class organization, blossomed out into a truly national institution.

The ambitious scope of the organization may be judged from the establishment, at the second congress of the Third International, of a bureau of International Proletcult, which included representatives from Austria, Belgium, England, France, Germany,

Italy, Norway, Russia, Switzerland, and the United States. In its
world appeal the bureau declared that, to date (April 12, 1920):

> The number of workers organized in Russian proletcults is not less than
> 400,000, of whom 80,000 have not merely joined the movement, but are
> taking an active part in its various studios. The state does not in the least
> delimit the proletcult, but values its full independence and lends it lavish
> aid. There are fifteen proletcult periodicals in Russia. The proletcult has
> published 10,000 copies of literary productions exclusively by proletarian
> authors. About three million musical compositions of various titles have
> been produced by proletarian composers. Proletarian painters and actors
> have also come to the fore.

The statement had a sanguine sound. Indeed, the year 1920 saw
the peak of proletcult growth. In 1922, the number of proletcult
units fell from three hundred to twenty, and in 1924 to seven. In
itself the centralization of effort might have been a sign of health,
had it not been for the parallel falling off of studio members: their
number was ten thousand in 1920, two thousand in 1922, and four
hundred and twelve in 1924. The flourishing phase of proletcult
coincided with the lowest ebb of public well-being in Russia—
years of civil war, intervention, blockade, famine, the period of
"military communism." Proletcult reflected the romantically heroic
notions, the half-baked extremism of the early stage of the revolution. The next stage meant sober reconstruction, under conditions
of comparative peace. The recrudescence of private enterprise under the NEP, the reappearance of private publishers and periodicals,
with the resulting free competition of talent, blasted the hothouse
plants that had been artificially nurtured and fostered. Furthermore, the government began to regard the proletcult more critically, and refused to tolerate the independence of a rival to the
Commissariat of Education. The organization dwindled, while the
educational work of the proletcult studios was taken over and carried on by regular institutions whose energy and breadth grew
with the country's recovery.

The tangible results of the proletcult activity were rather modest. About half a dozen prominent poets came out of the litstudios, and perhaps more than twice as many indifferent writers. As a rule, the successful "graduates" turned their backs upon their "alma mater," and banded in rival groups ("Smithy," "October," to be discussed a little farther on). But one cannot compute the beneficial effects of the movement on thousands of illiterate and semi-illiterate young people throughout the country. To be sure, these young people did not receive a specifically "proletarian culture"; rather they were initiated into the rudiments of "bourgeois" culture, be it the rules of prosody or simple arithmetic or the use of a handkerchief. They were lifted out of darkness and dumbness to a vision of humanity's finest creations of the mind and to a possibility of becoming articulate. This thrilling accomplishment lies outside the scope of my essay. More germane to this discussion are the proletcult *ideas,* which lingered on in varying aspects and produced heated debates long after the passing of the "boom."

Views of Voronsky and Trotsky.—The first contention of the proletcult and its successors was the need and inevitability of a proletarian culture and, in particular, of a proletarian literature. Bogdanov and his associates emphasized its desirability, while the more ardent enthusiasts referred to it as to an already existing phenomenon. On the extreme opposite side stood A. Voronsky (b. 1884), a Marxian critic and editor, and L. Trotsky. They denied not only the existence of a proletarian culture, but the very possibility of such a culture. The availability of a few proletarian scientists and artists does not make a class culture, so long as the class as a whole is not organically engaged in creating it. Trotsky defines culture as "an unfolded and inwardly coördinated system of knowledge and skill in all fields of material and spiritual creative effort." There can be no talk of a proletarian culture so long as the problem of the workers is how to lay hold of the extant bourgeois culture. Trotsky and Voronsky regarded contemporary Russian authors, even those of proletarian origin and communistic persuasion, as differing from bourgeois writers solely in ideology and purpose, but not in their literary art. As to the future, they saw no hope for the formation of a distinct proletarian culture, since during the "brief and transitory" period of proletarian dictatorship the workers will be too busy fighting for existence and the entrenchment of their power; and once the dictatorship is over, there will be no place for proletarian, or any class culture. "Hence," wrote Trotsky, "we must draw the general conclusion that not only is there no proletarian culture, but that there will be none, a fact which need not be regretted: the proletariat has taken over the power for the precise purpose of doing away forever with class culture, and paving the way for a human culture."

Trotsky's aptitude for reasoning in absolutes has made him subject to doctrinairism. Like his proletcult extreme opponents, he and Voronsky became enmeshed in terminology and its unqualified interpretation. One must be blind to deny that Soviet Russia has produced a relatively new culture, in its broadest sense. If the term "proletarian" is dubious, replace it by "revolutionary," or "socialist," or "sovietist," or "transitional," or any name that might suggest the shift of values from the individualistic and acquisitive plane to one of collectivism, with the profit motive eliminated. Trotsky discouraged the idea of creative effort on the part of workers during the dictatorship period, confining their task to apprenticeship in the bourgeois school. On the other hand, such an erstwhile "bourgeois" writer as V. Bryusov asserted that there "can and must be" a proletarian culture, pleading only for the coöperation of representatives of the old and the new, in order to produce a "synthesis" of the two—as every new culture in world history has been, invariably. Farther than Bryusov went the futurists in their clamor for a new art expressive of the new order; in their post-NEP garb, LEF, they entered into a formal alliance with the arch-proletarian group, MAPP (Moscow Association of Proletarian Writers, sub-

sequently merged with the RAPP). The constructivists followed
suit, in a similar formal alliance with the MAPP. Strange bed-
fellows they were, the vociferous proletarians and what these
called "the flotsam of bourgeois decadence," the formalistically
inclined poetic groups. What united them was the common conviction of the need of a *new* art. The word "proletarian" was used
rather loosely, but why quibble about a word that has been sanc-
tioned by usage?

Lunacharsky's Position.—The official attitude toward proletcult
and its derivatives gave the impression of vacillation; in any case,
it was vague enough to permit more than one interpretation, and
soft enough to be ignored when its meaning was clear beyond
doubt. This policy may be partly explained by the personality of
the Commissar of Education, Lunacharsky. For years before the
revolution he occupied a peculiar place in the Bolshevik faction,
as a man of genteel tastes, brilliant, urbane, somewhat bookishly
eloquent, and well known as an essayist on literature, music, the
theater, and art in general. He had been, in a sense, the ambassador
of uncouth bolshevism in the salons of the intelligentsia. During
the Capri School period, Lunacharsky provoked Lenin's contempt
for his Bogdanovist leanings and his flirtation with the mystic notions that reflected the disenchantment of the intelligentsia after
the abortive revolution of 1905. The slogan of the "Philosophical-
Religious Group" of Merezhkovsky was "God-seeking" (*bogoiska-
telstvo*); it expressed the desire of tired intellectuals to escape from
Marxian materialism into misty religiosity. To counteract this current, Lunacharsky coined a compromise, more "dynamic," term—
"God-building" (*bogostroitelstvo*), which was to serve as a challenge to create and build in union with the masses of the people,
"creator of all values," including religions. This idea, embodied in
Gorky's novel, *The Confession,* made Lenin squirm with chagrin
and disgust. In 1917, however, Lunacharsky was the only logical
person to take charge of "spiritual" matters, while the other leaders

engaged in a desperate fight for the very existence of the newborn state. As Commissar of Education, Lunacharsky faced the difficult task of diverting the channel of a heretofore exclusive culture of the few into the broad course of a popular and universally accessible culture. At the outset there was a shortage of personnel and facilities to satisfy the sudden clamor for knowledge on the part of the hitherto cowed millions. This unpreparedness was aggravated by the hostile attitude of the greater part of the intelligentsia, their reluctance to coöperate with the Bolsheviks, and their frequent sabotage. Furthermore, the Soviet Republic, universally hated and isolated from its very inception, was soon plunged into a life-and-death struggle on some sixteen fronts. All available man power was militarized. Such educated Russians as were too old or weak to be in the trenches had to grapple with a variety of problems in the rear, under conditions of hunger and cold. Visualize the great Pavlov (1849–1936) carrying on laboratory experiments, dressed in his fur coat, his fingers numb and stiff; Meierhold producing daring performances in unheated theaters; Glazunov raising his baton before a shivering orchestra and audience; sundry professors, novelists, poets, dancers, rushing from club to factory, from army barracks to college auditorium, to impart their knowledge and skill to emaciated, blue-lipped, but eager listeners and spectators.[4]

On the one hand, Lunacharsky had to battle saboteurs and open enemies of the new order, and on the other, he had to use tact in soliciting the coöperation of the "neutral" intelligentsia, the

---

[4] Here is a typical news item from the fall of 1919, when invading armies had practically surrounded the country, and the troops of General Yudenich were within an hour's march from Petrograd:

"In the literary section: In September and October regular classes of the litstudio met four times a week. . . . Lectures were read on prosody, on rhetoric, on the history of literature, on the theory of drama, on the history of material culture. In addition, K. Chukovsky read papers on Nekrasov [1821–1877], Gorky, and Walt Whitman. Maxim Gorky's lectures were postponed because of his illness. At the present moment nearly all the proletarian poets are at the front. Registration of new members continues."   The Petrograd *Gryadushcheye*, 7–8, 1919.

nonpolitical specialists, or "spets," as they came to be known in the abbreviated parlance of the new Russia. It goes without saying that he greeted with open arms the sympathizers who volunteered to work with the authorities, even when he had misgivings about the quality of the proffered help (as in the case of the futurists). Naturally, in his official capacity he could not help welcoming the formation of proletcult groups and offering them encouragement and support. The proletariat had just won its great victory and established a proletarian state, the functionaries of which were obviously expected to heed the demands of the ruling masses. Lunacharsky endeavored to be impartial in his protection of all intellectual and artistic groups that were willing to work under, and with, the Soviets. His tolerant catholicity was often abused and scorned, both by Bolshevik leaders who objected to his softness and by rival schools claiming superiority and demanding privileges.

Now and then, Lunacharsky was compelled to restrain publicly such groups and schools as went too far in their demands. He was especially sensitive on the question of the treatment of the old art. One of his most creditable achievements as commissar was the preservation of old monuments and works of art; owing to his zeal and vigilance, the Russian revolution was guilty of a minimum of vandalism. With a mixture of contempt and amusement, "rock-hard" Bolsheviks recall an incident from the early days of the October revolution, when their headquarters were still at the Petrograd Smolny Institute. Tears running down his cheeks, Lunacharsky rushed into the room where the council of commissars was in session, and handed in his resignation: he had just heard that the Bolshevik troops in Moscow had bombarded and partly demolished the Kremlin. The rumor proved false. He obviously resented the vandalistic attitude toward "bourgeois" art on the part of the extremists, whether these were futurists or proletcultists. In December, 1918, he addressed a Petrograd meeting, presided over by Mayakovsky, vigorously protesting against the wholesale dismissal of old art as bourgeois and therefore meriting discard. The only old art he agreed to be wary about was the "decadent art of the capitalistic bourgeoisie"—an obvious wink at all formalists. He went on to say: "We do not want to destroy monuments of the old art, and we shall permit no one to do that. . . . Let the proletariat choose the things that may be needful for its culture." About four months later he was constrained to take issue on the same subject with the overzealous proletarians who suffered from swellheadedness:

> In no case must the proletcult regard the first shoots of proletarian art and thought as ripe values, and attempt to substitute these for the cultural values of preceding epochs. Neither should the proletcult undertake to disseminate through its organs the entire body of "human knowledge." . . . The proletcult should center all its attention on studio activities.

For Lunacharsky, that was clear and strong. However, his enthusiasm for the educational work of the proletcult was apt to carry him off his feet and cause him to rhapsodize in the style of his "God-building" days. In the fall of 1919, he said in a speech at the Palace of Proletarian Culture:

> How many times during these years of hunger have I attended crowded openings of workers' theaters, and heard how now Shelley, now Pushkin, spoke to you. Those geniuses, who were ever eager to reach the hearts of the people, are at this sorrowful moment breaking in like a waft of sunshine at the windows of workmen's shanties, opened wide by the working class. . . . These geniuses are not yours, gentlemen of the bourgeoisie, but ours. Ours, not to be slavishly adored and blindly imitated. They are simply our comrades and fellow sufferers who shape and create life, as we are trying to do. Such geniuses must occupy a place of honor in our proletarian Pantheon, because they will yet contribute to the free creation of world culture, at the head of which the proletariat is now marching. It was once said that the foundation of one labor union is more important than the Battle of Sedan; surely the foundation and flourishing of proletcult groups in Soviet Russia is not less important than many a significant event in history. . . . The proletariat has risen as Man, with a capital letter. . . . He is, properly speaking, a Prometheus who opens new roads. This is

why at every proletarian festival, and here, in this Palace of Proletarian Culture, I feel as though I were at some special divine service in the name of future humanity.... The future historian will with a trembling hand inscribe the chronicle of our days in the great pages, and will perhaps with tears of tender emotion record the history of the proletcult, these first beginnings of a free, great, proletarian art.

Lenin's Attitude.—This "banquet speech" was not in Bolshevik style..It could hardly be palatable to Lenin, who had no patience with any "divinities" and did not relish exaggerated glorifications of workers' activities. Lunacharsky himself recorded in his reminiscences that Lenin had misgivings about the proletcult's "venturing" to form "proletarian science and proletarian culture": "That seemed to him, in the first place, an untimely and impossible task; in the second place, he thought that such half-ripe fantasies would divert the workers from studying; in the third place, he was apparently afraid lest some political heresy become imbedded in the proletcult. The big role played at the time in the proletcult by Bogdanov, for example, he treated with intense enmity." In writing and by word of mouth Lenin was quite outspoken in his contempt for overconfident proletarians bent on throwing into the dustbin whatever was not one hundred per cent proletarian. Here are excerpts from a speech of his in March, 1919:

The old utopian socialists imagined ... that first they would rear pretty, tidy, perfectly trained individuals, and then proceed to build socialism out of them. We have always laughed at that, as at doll play, a diversion for muslin-clad young ladies of socialism....

We are going to build socialism out of those very people who have been brought up by capitalism, spoiled and corrupted by it, but also tempered by it for battle. There are proletarians who are so tempered and hardened as to be capable of bearing sacrifices a thousand times more than any army. There are tens of millions of oppressed peasants, dark and scattered, but capable of uniting for struggle around the proletariat, under its skillful leadership. Then there are specialists in science, in technology, all of them thoroughly permeated by a bourgeois outlook.... We want to build socialism right away out of the material left over by capitalism, from yester-

day to today, at once, and not out of such individuals as may be prepared
in hothouses....

If you are not going to build a communistic society out of this available
material, you are empty phrasemongers, babblers....

We must take over the entire culture left from capitalism, and out of it
build socialism. We must take over all science, technology, all knowledge
and art. Without all that, we cannot build the life of a communistic society.
And that science, technology, art are in the hands and heads of specialists.

Such is the task we face in all fields, a contradictory task, as all capitalism is contradictory, a most difficult but feasible task.

One of these contradictions, and an obstacle for the proper education of the masses, Lenin saw in the abundance of survivors of
the bourgeois intelligentsia who had flooded workers' and peasants'
institutions, and under the guise of "purely proletarian art and
'proletarian culture'" had concocted "most absurd clowning" and
"supernatural silly nonsense." Speaking of this phenomenon in
May, 1919, Lenin made allowances for such a "drawback" as "natural and excusable for a vast movement in its early stage," but he
expressed his hope that the new state "was getting out, and would
get out, of that hole." The persistent demands to discard "old
values" on the part of proletarians and would-be proletarian "survivors of the bourgeois intelligentsia" compelled Lenin to return to
this theme again and again. In his *Infantile Disease of "Leftism"
in Communism,* published about one year after the last-quoted
speech, he reiterated his conviction that the absorption of the capitalist heritage by the proletariat was inevitable:

We can—and must—begin the building of socialism not out of some
fantastic human material especially manufactured by us, but out of what
we have inherited from capitalism. This is very "difficult," there is no
denying, but any other approach to the problem is so frivolous as not to
be worth talking about.

One may note, in passing, how the style betrays the man, in
Lenin's speech as much as in Lunacharsky's. Lenin minced no
words and was not squeamish about repeating himself when nec-

essary. In his address to the third conference of Communistic
Youth, in October, 1920, he reëmphasized his objection to light-
minded sneering at the old culture. He defined the task of all
youth, and especially of communistic youth, by one word: study.

But [he went on] you would make a huge mistake in concluding that one
may become a communist without absorbing all that which has been accumulated by human knowledge. It would be a mistake to think that it is
enough to master communistic watchwords, the conclusions of the science
of communism, without having mastered the sum of knowledge, of which
communism itself is but the outcome. Marxism is a sample of how communism emerged out of the sum of human knowledge.

After outlining the labor performed by Marx in critically uti-
lizing all extant human knowledge before he arrived at his own
conclusions, Lenin brought the point home:

We must bear this in mind when we discuss proletarian culture, for example. We cannot solve that problem without a clear understanding of
the fact that we can build a proletarian culture only by means of a precise
knowledge of the culture created by the whole development of humanity,
and by means of its adaptation. Proletarian culture must not be expected
to leap out of nowhere, it cannot be realized as the invention of persons
who call themselves specialists of proletarian culture. All this is sheer nonsense. Proletarian culture cannot be anything but a normal development
of the stores of knowledge amassed by mankind under the oppression of
a capitalist society, a landowners' society, a bureaucratic society.

At the sessions of the first all-Russian congress of proletcults,
Lenin had a private talk with Lunacharsky, and apparently urged
him to impress upon the congress the need of greater modesty and
more conformity with reality. The next day Lenin read in the
Izvestiya ("News") a report of Lunacharsky's speech at the congress, the sentiment of which seemed to be "in direct contrast"
(according to Lenin) to what the two had agreed upon in their
preceding conversation. Among other things, Lunacharsky promised "a guaranty of complete autonomy for proletcult." Lenin's
patience with the all-too-gentle, temperamental commissar was ex-

hausted. He immediately drafted a resolution, and urged its endorsement "with extraordinary speed" by the Central Committee of the Party, the Commissariat of Education, and the proletcult congress. In clear terms the resolution stated the need of spreading Marxian education among the people, and the imperative duty of following the example of Marx by critically absorbing whatever is of value in the past. The final clause signified that the hesitating policy of the government was to be done away with once and for all:

The all-Russian congress of proletcult most resolutely rejects as theoretically false and practically harmful all attempts to invent a peculiar culture, to shut oneself in exclusive organizations, to delimit the field of activity of the Commissariat of Education and of the proletcult, or to establish the "autonomy of proletcult within the Commissariat's institutions. On the contrary, the congress deems it the absolute duty of all proletcult organizations to consider themselves as fully subordinate organs in the net of the Commissariat's institutions, and to carry on their work, as part of the tasks of proletarian dictatorship, under the general guidance of the Soviet authorities (particularly the Commissariat of Education).

Lunacharsky had yielded on the question of autonomy, one may surmise, under the persistent onslaught of its advocates. Here, again, the futurists and proletcultists struck a common note. The *Art of the Commune* (an organ of the Commissariat!) sneered at the idea of a link of continuity between the old and the new art, demanded a leftist dictatorship of the arts, and accused the authorities of being "conciliators in matters pertaining to cultural activities, especially to art." In Bolshevik parlance the word "conciliator" stood for what was regarded just short of treason. The Petrograd Comfut, an ephemeral communist-futurist group, branded in its first declaration the Commissariat of Education as opportunist and as incapable of "counteracting the age-old power of bourgeois ideologues." As to the proletcult, it insisted from the very beginning on carrying on its work independently of the government, arguing that the latter represented heterogeneous groups and classes and could not be entrusted with an activity that was to be one hundred

per cent proletarian. Time and again, leading proletcult units, like
the Moscow center, voted against submitting to the control of the
Commissariat of Education. Lunacharsky weakened, and gave in.

Lenin's personal interference brought immediate results. At its
final session the congress passed a resolution to make the proletcult
a section of the Commissariat of Education; this was a mild form
of hara-kiri. The year 1920 ended with a lengthy declaration by
the Central Committee of the Party, which embodied the points
of Lenin's draft resolution concerning the proletcult, and contained
a few illuminating "explanations." It pointed out that the first
proletcult was organized under the Kerensky (b. 1881) regime,
when quite naturally it desired to be independent of the official
Ministry of Education. After the Bolshevik Revolution there remained no reason for claiming independence from a *workers'*
government, yet the proletcult continued to maintain this line of
isolation. For this and other reasons, various "socially alien elements" managed to wedge into the organization: "futurists, decadents, adherents of the anti-Marxian idealistic philosophy, and
lastly, just ne'er-do-wells from the ranks of bourgeois publicists and
philosophers began here and there to take charge of proletcult
affairs." These intelligentsia elements interfered with the educational progress of the proletarian youth, by imposing on it "semi-
bourgeois philosophical 'systems' and fancies." The declaration
linked these misleading ideas with those of the "social-democratic
intelligentsia" in the reactionary years of 1907–1912, hinting rather
transparently at Bogdanov and Lunacharsky. Half apologetically
the declaration further explained that the Party had been prevented
by wars from showing its interest in the matter earlier. From now
on the Party was going "to pay far greater attention to questions
of popular education in general, and to proletcult in particular." It
proceeded to explain that, as part of the Commissariat, proletcult
groups would not lose any of their privileges and autonomy in the
field of creative work: the Party would see to it that the cause of

workers' culture should be handled by actual "workers' intelligentsia." The declaration concluded by mercilessly lashing Lunacharsky's equivocal policy:

> The Central Committee is aware of the fact that the same intelligentsia
> currents that showed a disintegrating influence on the proletcult have
> made themselves felt up to now in the Commissariat of Education itself.
> The Central Committee aims to remove these bourgeois elements from
> the Commissariat. . . .

It further promised to sift carefully the educational personnel in
the provinces, so that their coöperation with proletcults might help
the Party to raise the level of the work of enlightenment and to
"lend to the activity of the Commissariat a genuinely proletarian
character."

The final dismissal of Lunacharsky and his replacement (in
1929) by a more dependable Party man, Bubnov (b. 1883), did not
take place for another decade or so. But the proletcult as an organization was dealt a decisive blow and merely lingered on for a few
more years as a shadow of its former self. Yet its basic ideas persisted, and reëmerged under various guises, in spite of Lenin's
intense attacks and repeated official condemnations. Most stubborn
in persistence was the notion of a distinct proletarian literature, its
superiority, and its deserved priority in the graces of a workers'
state. This line of reasoning can be traced through successive
groups from "Smithy" and "October" to MAPP and RAPP, up
to their official disbandment in 1932.

In the fall of 1922, *Pravda,* the official organ of the Party, opened
its pages to a discussion of the ever-burning problem of proletarian
culture and proletcult. Among the leading articles one should note
one by V. Pletnev (b. 1886), chairman of the proletcult central
committee, and its rebuttal, by Y. Yakovlev. The relevance of that
polemic was accentuated after the death of Lenin (January, 1924),
when his utterances acquired an indisputable weight. Among the
leader's papers was found the issue of *Pravda* that contained Plet-

nev's contribution, interspersed with Lenin's marks and notations. Furthermore it was made clear, in 1925, that Yakovlev's concluding article of the discussion had been inspired by Lenin and approved by him. One obtained thus a direct glimpse of Lenin's final views on the debatable question, views which no orthodox member of the Party would dare gainsay. The matter therefore merits a brief comment.

Pletnev was a proletarian, a communist, a man trusted by the leaders, as may be seen from the fact of his having been placed at the head of the reformed proletcult. Indeed, Pletnev sharply rejected Bogdanov's vague views, and as against the demand for full autonomy he emphatically approved of proletcult submission to the control of the government and the Party. Nevertheless, in his exposition of the aims and tasks of the new proletcult, Pletnev unwittingly reiterated Bogdanov's basic principles, a defection which could not escape Lenin's keen eye. Thus, Pletnev's sentence: "The creation of a new proletarian class culture is the basic aim of proletcult," evoked Lenin's "ha-ha!" in the margin. Furthermore, the words "creation," "new," and "basic" were ironically underlined twice. In the same eloquently laconic manner Lenin queried Pletnev's other contentions, now underlining a passage once or twice, now boxing a word or a phrase, now scribbling a row of question marks, now jotting a "hm!" or "rubbish!" or "what a mess!" or "oof!" Pletnev was guilty of what Lenin regarded as a mortal sin, for which he coined the word *komchvanstvo,* "comsnobbery," denoting the aristocratic sense of superiority and almightiness on the part of dizzy-headed communists. Pletnev expressed utter distrust of the bourgeois intelligentsia and of the peasantry, doubting the possibility that a nonproletarian scientist, artist, engineer, or clerk could be loyal to the new order. According to his dialectics "bourgeois class culture is the thesis; its antithesis is proletarian culture; and only beyond the threshold of class society, under socialism, lies their synthesis—all-human culture." In order to conquer the cultural heights, a relentless class war must be waged, "any *Burgfriede* being out of the question." Proletarian culture must be built "only by proletarian forces, by scientists, artists, engineers, and others, who have come out of the proletariat." Opposite this sentence Lenin inscribed in the margin: "arch-fiction."

In his lengthy article Yakovlev summed up Lenin's views on the problem, their essence being in effect that in a land as backward and illiterate as Russia the immediate task consists in raising the masses to the cultural level of the European and American middle class. This is a gigantic task, and the proletariat is not strong enough to accomplish it: "Russia's working class, families included, hardly comprises fifteen per cent of the population, and the Communist Party contains less than ten per cent of the proletariat." Yakovlev recommended the dismissal of high-sounding phrases and unattainable ambitions, in favor of a sober and prolonged effort at an elementary general schooling of the masses.

Lenin denied neither the desirability nor the possibility of a proletarian culture, as Trotsky had done. He tried to hammer into the heads of "comsnobs" the necessity of first acquiring the prerequisites for such a culture, namely, the elements of general, "bourgeois" culture. This may sound obvious now, but in those feverish days Lenin was prompted again and again to emphasize the inevitably slow tempo that must be used in this process:

The cultural problem cannot be solved as rapidly as political or military problems. . . . During an acute crisis one may win politically in a few weeks. In war one may win in a few months, but cultural victories are not possible in so short a time. Here a much longer time is needed by the very nature of the case, and for this longer time we must adjust ourselves by displaying the maximum of pertinacity, insistence, and systematism. . . .

As a revolutionist Lenin possessed the rare combination of resolute aggressiveness and a clear head. This explains his unswerving course of action in the years 1917–1920, when some of his associates lost heart and were ready to give up. This also explains Lenin's flexibility and willingness to yield to the demands of reality, as he did in 1921, with the introduction of the NEP. He was fond of quoting Goethe's aphorism about the golden-green tree of life as against gray theory.[5] Having no illusions about the backwardness of the country, he was endeavoring to "spur Russia to her haunches" (in the words of Pushkin about Peter the Great); he realized, without losing his sobriety and clearheadedness, the paramount importance of raising the intelligence of the people. The core of the issue is presented most lucidly in the following lines, taken from Lenin's article "On Coöperation":

Our opponents have told us more than once that we are undertaking the senseless job of implanting socialism in an insufficiently cultured country. They have overlooked the fact that we started from a different end from the one prescribed by the theories of sundry pedants; that with us the political and social revolution happens to precede the cultural revolution, which we are facing at the moment.

This cultural revolution is all we need now in order to become a fully socialistic country. But for us this revolution presents unbelievable difficulties, both cultural, because we are illiterate, and material, since culture presupposes a certain development of the material means of production, a certain material basis.

It took another ten years for the simple truth of Lenin's views to become a guide in Soviet policies regarding cultural matters. Comsnobbism—or, more broadly, proletsnobbism—proved a malignant ailment; time and effort were required to eradicate it from Soviet life. One must also remember that as long as the new order faced enemies on every side and was uncertain of its stability, it could ill afford to ignore those who claimed to be the spokesmen of its main pillar and defender, the working class. Up to the end of 1920 the state was surrounded by hostile armies, and upon the inauguration of the NEP, in 1921, it encountered an inner enemy in the form of a recrudescent bourgeoisie.

---

[5] "Grau, teurer Freund, ist alle Theorie,
Und grün des Lebens goldner Baum."
                                    Schülerszene, Faust I.

The "Smithy" Group

The first secession from proletcult took place in 1920, with the formation of the group "Smithy" (*Kuznitsa*), composed of poets and novelists who had come out of the working masses, and most of whom had appeared in print before the revolution. As far as actual creative writing goes, and not mere declarations and platforms, the "Blacksmiths" were the most productive group of proletarian authors. Shades of ideological and tactical differences caused them to split a number of times and to join or form other groups. Such a group as "Defile" (*Pereval*), a band of proletarian and non-proletarian writers, naturally differed from the "Smithy" both in composition and tendencies. On the other hand, such groups as "Cosmist," "Create!," "Workers' Spring," were kindred enough to be almost identical, except in name. The rivalry between "Smithy" and "October," with such of its allies as "Young Guard," MAPP, VAPP, and RAPP ("Moscow," "All-Russian," "Russian Association of Proletarian Writers," respectively), was, as we shall presently see, primarily of a tactical nature.

"Defile" excepted, the other groups professed essentially similar views, with slight variations, and harked back to Bogdanov's fundamentals. Thus, they all accepted Bogdanov's point about the organizational function of literature. The "Smithy" defined the aim of proletarian literature as "the aspiration to transform the chaos of life into an organized force capable of developing in a planned way." No less abstract and general sounded the wording of "October," in assigning to proletarian literature the role of "organizing the psyche and the consciousness of the working class." They likewise agreed in demanding hegemony for proletarian writers and in scorning all other contemporary writers. Formalism, preoccupation with form for its own sake, was rejected by all of them; they recognized the primacy of content over form and the need of accord between the two. Bogdanov's doctrine of a critical absorption of the "heritage" was whittled down to an admission that the proletariat might learn some technical methods from other cultures, with reservations. Of course, each group claimed to be the only full-fledged and revolutionary alliance of worker-authors, and regarded the claims of other groups as preposterous.

An interesting study could be made of the style and verbiage of these "proletarian" declarations, which more often than not betrayed a bourgeois origin, symbolist or futurist or imagist or constructivist or a melange of all these and more. There was as little modesty or moderation about the proletarian announcements as about the nonproletarian counterparts. Quite often their cocksureness and braggadocio suggest the bliss of ignorance. In its 1923 declaration the "Smithy" defines proletarian art as "an art which encompasses the three-dimensional field of creative material in a clear, precise, synthetic form corresponding to the [working] class. . . . By its very nature it is an art of big canvases and grand style, a monumental art." A contemporary critic, V. Polonsky (1886–1932), treated this definition with ironic reserve:

> For ages preproletarian aesthetics attempted, with the aid of great minds, to answer the question, What is art? To this day mankind has found no indisputable answer. But it has an *art,* which somewhat reconciles us to the absence of an absolute definition of art. In our case the position is reversed: as yet there is no proletarian art, but the "Blacksmiths" together with other comrades have declaratively proclaimed the definition of proletarian art.

Kazin.—Most literary manifestoes are replete with abstractions and generalities that are seldom sustained or illustrated by the actual output of the harbingers. The proletarians present no exception to this rule. The few points for which they do furnish concrete examples are worth noting. The motive of labor, for instance. One of the founders of "Smithy," Lyashko (b. 1884), declares:

> What chiefly unites proletarian writers is the sense of work, the feeling that only through work will the ideal be attained . . . , that work is the

measurement of justice, of equality. Even phenomena of nature they endow with labor processes. The moon, trills of nightingales, stars, the sun, the cuckoo—all these evoke labor images in proletarian writers.

This much is undoubtedly true. The one definite contribution of proletarian poets may be found in the freshness and newness of some of their similes and images. On occasion they enliven the most hackneyed subject matter by an unexpected approach. Typical of this approach is Vasily Kazin (b. 1898). A workman and the son of a workman, Kazin sees everything through the prism of physical labor. When he muses on the blonde who had once jilted him and with whom he is about to have a tryst, the threadbare theme receives an original turn in the worker-poet's address to his tool:

> Livelier, jack plane, scrape faster,
> Swish, sing over the bench,
> Curry the plank with hot steel,
> With your steely hot comb.
> Ah, flurry, flutter to the ground,
> You, fair curls, off the board!
> Hey, has not some honey dripped on you?
> How fragrant you are, how sweet!
> Do you recall her, O jack plane,
> Saying good-bye to us in a hurry?
> Tossing her curls,
> Pompously rustling the shavings?
> That moment with sharp pain a splinter
> Drove deep into my heart,
> And you, on our parting,
> Lay deep under dust.
> Lo, today the clang of our tryst—
> And you, curling swift coils,
> Flurry up warm memories
> Of those beloved curls.
> Livelier, jack plane, scrape faster,
> Swish, sing over the bench,
> Curry the plank with hot steel,
> With your steely hot comb.

Kazin sees the sun with the eyes of a bricklayer ("morning hoisted his brick"), while the coming of spring he perceives in terms of a tin roofer, and evening is to him an apiarist whose bees are stars. A thunderstorm is thus refracted on his retina:

THE HEAVENLY FOUNDRY

Both tall and vast
The bluestone foundry.
Hush! The fitful siren
Summons in dusty tones.
From all ends speed
In thick smudgy blouses
Throngs of mighty blacksmiths,
Welded by the windful siren.
Ever darker, darker the height.
Came together the dark throngs
And nimbly
They set aflame
Furnaces of lightnings,
And with a reverberating blow
The foundry's vastness they shook.

Machine and Iron.—The poet Gerasimov's carpenters and miners also envisage nature in their particular professional way. Workmen with a nostalgia for the village see things with the eyes of Sannikov (b. 1899), who hears the calls of the cuckoo in the strokes of the hammer on the anvil, and whom the factory siren reminds of the sunrise song of the rooster. Hundreds of similarly novel metaphors sound natural, quite unbookish, and give one the feeling that their authors are in their element. Less spontaneous appear the poems that glorify modern industry and its mechanical features. In these one is more often than not aware of a made-to-order, programmatic note. Like Marinetti, the "Smithy" sings hymns to the machine. "Machinism, the metallic theme," the "Blacksmiths" regard as another "distinctive feature of proletarian literature"; they are expected to "penetrate into the soul of metal, into its history, into its intimate world and character."

That was a new note, just as industry was a comparative new-comer in Russia. In the West the industrial proletariat has had ample time to work out a specific psychology and world outlook, whereas in Russia before the revolution the great majority of factory workers were erstwhile peasants. Forced into the city by poverty, heavy taxation, exhaustion of the soil, insufficiency of allotments, which moreover he cultivated in the most backward manner, and by periodic famines, the peasant entered the factory as an inferno. He hated and feared the "iron tyrant," and constantly longed for the green spaces of the countryside which he loved in spite of starvation conditions. These sentiments were much in evidence in the poetry of proletarian poets until the advent of "October" turned everything topsy-turvy, including the worker's attitude toward the factory and the machine. The "iron tyrant" overnight became the "iron messiah" (the phrase is Kirillov's), the enslaving machine revealed its opposite aspect, its mission of a liberator.

An avalanche of hymns to industrial labor burst forth, of hosannahs to giant furnaces and tall factory vaults, of hallelujahs to granite and concrete, and above all to iron, iron, iron. In a variety of forms and meters obviously borrowed from nonproletarian poets (such as the democratic radicals Whitman and Verhaeren), they now sang praises to yesterday's "inferno" and its cleansing labor. Thus Sadofyev:

> Day after day to be in the foundry, to be in the foundry—is a delight.
> To understand the iron language, to listen to mysteries, revelations,
> From machines, lathes, to learn the fierce power—to destroy,
> The radiant new other power—incessantly to create.

N. Vladimirov was convinced that the freed workers would "transform the factories into life-giving temples of the soul," while for I. Yonov (b. 1887) the factory was the anteroom of a new and perfect life:

> O great, eternal labor! Glory to thee who hast cleansed
> Russia, us, in the forge's crucible;
> Who with an imperious hand hast merged into one beat
> The heart's soft throb and the thunder of the anvil.
> 'Tis likely that some of us, beneath the weight of the blow,
> May fall amid the rumble and clatter of lathes,
> But the more unisonally with zeal of muscle and steam
> We will turn earthy the patterns of gorgeous dreams.
> To the song of keen drills, the whistle of steam engines,
> We will jointly lead up our stubborn labor
> To the moment when, to the sound of other tunes,
> We shall march by a new road to a new order.

Obviously influenced by the melodiousness of Balmont and the cold urbanity of Bryusov, V. Kirillov poured his new wine into old skins:

> I have overheard these songs of oncoming joyous ages
> In the sonorous whirlwind of fiery-faced vast cities.
> I have discerned these songs of golden future days
> In the roar of factories, in screams of steel, angry swish of belts.
> I watched my comrade forge golden steel,
> And in that very nick I surmised the wondrous face of Pending Dawn:
> I have learned that all world's wisdom is inclosed in this my hammer,
> In this firm and stubborn and sure hand.
> The harder this hammer will strike, forge, crush,
> The brighter joy will shine in this gloomy world;
> The more nimbly will gears and pinions move,
> The more enchanting and radiant our days will flare forth. . . .
> These songs were sung for me by millions of voices,
> By millions of blue-bloused, strong, bold blacksmiths.
> These songs are a mighty summons to the sun, to life and struggle,
> They are a challenge inflexible to malignant, irksome fate.

Gerasimov.—More direct and authentically proletarian are the verses of M. Gerasimov, an itinerant worker and globetrotter, who knew well the insides of Russian and Western European mines, automobile and metallurgical plants, and also had a taste of jails and trenches. The following poem may not be strictly autobiographical, but it epitomizes the formative elements of the "iron muse" of Gerasimov and of other poets in that vein:

> I am not tender, I am not from a hothouse,
> No need to treat me gently:
> In a husky foundry, beneath a machine,
> My mother gave me birth.
> Singeing, whipping flame
> Hung over me.
> An electric nipple
> I greedily sucked with my lips.
> A steel cradle rocked me,
> I was lulled by the buoyant siren.
>
> . . .
>
> Over my bed the dynamo, like a wolf,
> Bared its fiery tusks;
> Molten metal gurgled,
> Howl and roar whirled.
> In the inveterate oaths
> Of pinions and shafts
> I heard friendly sounds,
> A maternal call.
> Only the men in blue
> Called me "son."
> Their genial faces I'll ever remember.
> Laughingly they handed me toys:
> Cylinders, a connecting rod, a flywheel.
> I played with a two-ton hammer.
> At one month I had cut my teeth;
> Mother's milk was rusty
> From blood and iron.

Similarly personal and at the same time typical of his class are Gerasimov's poems of the cycle "Iron Blossoms." His lyrical yearnings are forced into the grim grooves of a laborer's life. How does nature appear to one who emerges from deep in a Belgian mine?

> Together with the coal we were vomited by the mine.
> Night—black as the day underground.
> Twilight was finishing its watch
> By the dying furnace.
> Rainclouds wandered like miners
> Across mines of slaty heights,
> And the stars—lamps amid waste dumps—
> Lit the pockmarked vaults.

Or, again, has it ever occurred to us, while enjoying a sea voyage, what might be the reveries of a stoker?

> I am a stoker in the womb of a ship,
> In the cast-iron belly at the turbines,
> Where the heat of the sprayers is smoky and sickening,
> Where steam is my slave and my master.
>
> Amid the coral convolutions of slag,
> Within the steel pincers of fire bars,
> Where even black coke wept tears,
> There I lived clamped by chains of steel.
>
> Incessantly, through the ventilating pipes,
> The free wind trumpets its horn,
> It kisses one's parched lips,
> Now tender, now challengingly severe.
>
> All around, in azure space,
> In the hissing sparks of foamy waters,
> Lissom in their carefree journey,
> Dolphins dance in chorus.
>
> At night the water glimmers phosphorescent.
> Passion pierces you like an electric current.
> Kisses ring in the waves, inside the cabins,
> The whole world is languid with love.
>
> While here—bent backs
> Laden with coal, with slag and steel.
> Oh, to be like dolphins in the waves,
> Free from stokeholes and turbines,
> Off to speed into the miragey far-away!

With such a background, Gerasimov was quite in his element in the "iron" phase of Soviet poetry. Yet even his later verse sounds somewhat labored, bent on proving some point or other in the platform of "Smithy." This is felt in his long *Electropoem,* where along with magnificent images and powerful lines one comes upon arid reasoning and theorizing. The poem is an ambitious picture of the sweeping transformation of rural Russia by electric and electrifying labor. A mixture of genuine inspiration with bookish rhetoric appears also in his "In the Font of Iron," another hymn to the beautifying power of mechanized labor, with its concluding lines:

> The foundry—a cruel cataract.
> Copper, iron, ore stream forth—
> Electroflaming currents—
> Into labor's steely muscles.
> Each man becomes a fiery bard
> Of forging peals, of red strings,
> A thunderstormwinged titan,
> A tribune of the Dawn of the Future.

Gastev.—The poet Gastev, like Kirillov, Lyashko, and Gerasimov, began to write before the war and was one of the contributors to the proletarian anthology edited by Gorky in 1914. A metal worker, Gastev has given voice to a unique poetization of the metal foundry. Most of his compositions are in Whitmanesque free verse or in poetic prose. This style is well suited to his metallic rhapsodies of giant furnaces and rhythmic movements of men and machines. With an intimate knowledge of his material, Gastev animates, one might say anthropomorphizes, the plant and its marvelously functioning machinery. The huge crane manipulated by one workman, at whose will tons of metal, beams and cauldrons, are switched about, soaring beneath high vaults, becomes a splendid, powerful intelligence. What the constructivists tried to express in vague and obscure phrases about the "maximal exploitation of the theme," and "a system of functional justification of all the component artis-

tic elements," Gastev performed of his own accord, guided by no
-ism. His preoccupation with the "iron" theme narrowed his field
of vision, to be sure, but no one can doubt the genuineness of
Gastev's approach. Unfortunately this could not be said of his numerous imitators, some of whom substituted loudness for poetry—
the school of "screamism" (*vizgism*)—while others tried to pour
the "iron" motive into the mellifluousness of Balmont's verse,
with such saccharine results as these lines by Kirillov:

> There are calls in iron,
> Melodiously stormy.
>
> . . .
>
> There is purity in iron,
> Enticement, the radiance
> Of mimosa-tender eyelashes;
> There are trills of a flute,
> They flare up and die
> In the smiles of raptured faces.
> There is tenderness in iron,
> Playful snowiness,
> Love glimmers in its polish;
> The crimson of sunsets,
> Impulse and languor,
> Blood in its rusty curve.

A young offspring of the proletcult, A. Bezymensky (b. 1898),
though a follower of Mayakovsky, voiced the machinist vogue
in his "Word Foundry":

> Our soul is a foundry.
> Our heart, a living furnace.
> Our thoughts, a swishing belt.
> Our verse, a printer's galley.
> New builders
> Shall be
> Made ready.
> Hear you hums,
> Working
> Words?

Hear you life's call:
"Hey, to wo-o-o-rk!"?
Life's factory will supply ours
With ore,
And heaps
Of raw material
Will shoot them down our nerves—open roads.
Nothing in the universe is old rubbish!!
All that has been told,
All that has been chewed up,
We shall once more
Forge as new,
Shall speak in an iron, as yet unspoken, word,
Shall kindle with our fire.

Small wonder that even proletcultists could not stomach such a generous dose of "ironism," and one of them (Kiselev) addressed Gastev with a somewhat sarcastic parody:

Iron, iron, iron,
Furnaces, screws.
Oh, Gastev, you're forging poems
Out of verses of iron.
Iron, iron, iron,
You've entangled us in iron.
Iron is the roar of the *Marseillaise,*
Iron the sobs of Parnassus.
Iron, iron, iron,
Iron—whichever way you look!
Entangled is our poetry!
Ah, heavy are these iron days!!!

Gastev was not content with composing poetry in verse and prose; like so many of his contemporaries, he felt it his duty to theorize and preach. His views occupy an interesting place among proletarian platforms and programs. He envisaged the new proletariat, its psychology and culture, as a reflection of modern industry:

Great plants, tubes, pillars, bridges, cranes, and all the complex constructiveness of new buildings and concerns, their catastrophism and inex-

orable dynamics—these permeate the everyday consciousness of the proletariat. The whole life of modern industry is saturated with movement,
catastrophe; is framed into organized and strict regularity. Catastrophe
and dynamics chained by a grandiose rhythm—such is the fundamental
inspiring element of proletarian psychology.

Gastev believed in the universality of proletarian traits acquired
by dint of daily contact with the machine:

The machinization not only of gestures, not only of production methods, but of everyday thinking, coupled with extreme objectivity, normalizes
in a striking degree the psychology of the proletariat. We boldly assert
that no class, either of the old or of the modern world, has been pervaded
by such a normalized psychology as has the proletariat. No matter where
he may be working, in Germany, in San Francisco, in Australia, in Siberia,
the proletarian responds only to certain common psychological formulas
which perceive with the rapidity of an electric current a primary hint of
industry, and this they proceed to perfect into a complex of an intricate
pattern. True enough, as yet there is no international language, but there
are international gestures, international psychological formulas common
to millions. It is this that lends proletarian psychology such a striking
anonimity, which permits the qualification of separate proletarian units
as A, B, C, or as 325,075, or as 0, and the like. In this normalization of
psychology and in its dynamism is the key to the prodigious elemental-
ness of proletarian thinking. . . . In this psychology, from one end of the
world to the other, flow potent massive streams, making for one world
head in place of millions of heads. This tendency will next imperceptibly
render individual thinking impossible, becoming the objective psychology
of a whole class, with systems of psychological switches and locks.

Gastev proceeds to point out how the complexity of modern
industry, the interrelation and interdependence of multiple opera-
tions, their mutual control and subordination, affect the proletarian
psychology in a peculiar way, producing a "mechanized collectivism." "The manifestations of such mechanized collectivism are so
foreign to personalism, are so anonymous, that as these collectives-
complexes move they resemble the movement of objects, with individual human faces gone, as it were, showing instead normalized

footsteps, faces without expression, a soul stripped of lyricism, emotions gauged not by outcries, not by laughter, but by a manometer and a taxometer." "Is it not clear," he naïvely asks, "that in the proletariat we have a growing class which unfolds simultaneously a living working force, the iron mechanics of a new collective, and a new mass engineering that transforms the proletariat into an unheard-of social automaton?"

It is only natural that when a class with such an extraordinary psychology comes to power, it must create a new culture, a new art. On this point Gastev shows no such machinelike precision. He merely states, and italicizes, that *"with proletarian art we must associate an astounding revolution of art methods."* In literature, specifically, the word will have to be reformed, but not just "grammatically"—what the futurists have done; Gastev is willing "to risk the technicalization of the word." He does not predict the forms this technicalization may take, but he suggests that the word "will gradually be divorced from its living carrier, man." "We are coming close," he claims, "to a genuinely new amalgamated art, in which purely human demonstrations, pitiful modern mimicry, and chamber music will retreat to the background. We are moving toward an unprecedented objective demonstration of things, of mechanized crowds, and an overwhelming sheer grandiosity that knows nothing intimate and lyrical."

Gastev's mechanism not only produces a vague and decadent formalism in art; it robs the worker of all individual action and thought, and reduces him to an anonymous automaton, a robot. In his extremism Gastev was alone. He showed unintentionally to what absurd lengths machinism may lead. The stage of industrial romanticism was natural in a land with a new and limited industry the nationalization of which augured boundless possibilities. Most of the poets sang hymns to the machine, not as Gastev's depersonalizing monster but as a Prometheus, freeing man from the drudgery of toil and enabling him to conquer nature and harness it to

his will. All of them, however, narrowed the scope by glorifying
human endeavor, labor, in only one of its aspects, the physical—
manual or mechanized,—implying the inferiority of mental and
artistic efforts, as "nonproletarian." It need hardly be said that
such naïve notions did not endure beyond the early phase of the
revolution.

Collectivism and Planetarity.—Another feature regarded by the
"Blacksmiths" as distinctive of proletarian literature is "collectivism and planetarity." The latter idea, astronomically used rather
loosely, was evident in the name of a Petrograd group, "Cosmist,"
and in the cosmic swing of the poems and prose declarations of the
time. The word "collective," both as noun and adjective, appeared
nearly as often as "foundry" in the workers' verse of that period.
Sadofyev, Loginov (b. 1891), Alexandrovsky (b. 1897), and a host
of others sang of the "collective soul," of the "thought and will of
the collective," of "power kindled by the fire of the collective," of
the "collectively created Poem of Poems." In "Universal Comrade"
Sadofyev uses the word lavishly:

> With the plow of collective thought
> We shall raise the virgin soil, we shall plow it.
> We shall inebriate it with wondrous ecstasy—
> Better than paradise, finer than the sun. . . .
> . . . With the unrelenting effort
> Of Collective Labor
> We had built temples to Apollo,
> We have erected cities. . . .
> Conquering dark chaos,
> We rule the world collectively.

In their declarations the "Blacksmiths" emphasized their replacement of "I" by "we," not as a denial of individuality but in
token of its "congeniality" with the collective. The proletarian
sings of world labor, past, present, and future, of its unity in diversity: "The factory siren—a song summoning to work the work-

ers of many lands. At one and the same hour tens of millions of workers take hold of their tools, start their lathes, their machines, and in sounds of labor they sing a song to the future." There is enough sentiment here to place such poetry apart from Gastev's "mechanized collectivism." The line of demarcation between "I" and "we" becomes rather nebulous in the "Smithy's" literary tenets, as in this one, for example:

Whatever the subject matter of a composition by a worker—the steppe, forest, field, song, foundry, love,—at its base lies anxiety, pain, joy for the collective of the factory, the city, the country, the whole world. Behind the experiences of the individual, of the hero, one is aware of the collective, as though the individual had soaked it in fully.

This tenet, one may recall, was one of Bogdanov's fundamentals. The effect his teaching might have on budding literary critics can be exemplified by his enthusiastic comment on V. Torsky-Tsarev's verses, "Morning" and "Autumn." Though a worker, Torsky-Tsarev wrote in a sweetish philistine style, lacrimose and hackneyed, but Bogdanov extolled him because "the poet sees in the forest a collective, its various elements variously reacting to nature's phenomena." Torsky-Tsarev's melancholy birches recalling the "brightly colorful spring," "the aromatic adornments of fragrant flowers and grasses," move Bogdanov deeply, for the reason, as he says, that therein "nature is perceived through the eyes of a *collectivist.* His symbols show the *common* experience of a forest, not the individual experience of some one birch or pine, as in ordinary lyrics."

Form.—In regard to form, the "Blacksmiths" and their kindred did not claim any distinctly proletarian variety, unless it be Gastev's "technicalization of the word," an idea avowedly embryonic. Proletarian poetry has been eclectic in form and has contributed nothing original in the field. We have noted the influence of practically all preceding schools on the young singers. In the first years, Balmont, Bryusov, Bely, and Blok were felt here and there in the workers' verse, later alternating with Mayakovsky and Aseyev, futurists, and Yesenin, Kusikov (b. 1896), and other imagists. In a 1922 declaration the "Smithy" stated that while "ideologically the proletarian writers presented relatively one whole, in regard to form they differed according to their individual peculiarities." In subsequent declarations, especially in those emanating from "October" and its variants, emphasis was laid on realism as the most suitable form for proletarian art. A "Back to Pushkin!" movement was started, as opposed to the early futurist slogan, "Overboard with Pushkin from the steamer of modernity!" Nonrealism was decidedly in retreat about the middle of the nineteen-twenties: imagism gave up the ghost after the death of Yesenin, futurism limped on, desperately trying to lift its face, now as LEF, now as New LEF, finally as REF, while its offspring, constructivism, was represented, strictly speaking, by one poet, Selvinsky.

The question of form, of the "how" of the literary quality and tendency, was inevitably connected with the attitude of the proletarians toward nonproletarian art. Grudgingly admitting that they had a few things to learn from bourgeois "specialists," as far as "technique" was concerned, the proletarian spokesmen cautioned against the danger of ideological contamination. "Style is the class," proclaimed the "Blacksmiths"; hence the new order marked by the domination of the working class could not be expressed in the old style: "Artists crystallized under prerevolutionary conditions of life are powerless to put into form the material plowed up by the earthquake of the October revolution." Diagnosing the schools of symbolism, futurism, and imagism as convulsions of the dying capitalistic order, the "Blacksmiths" concluded that "yesterday's art of the word has degenerated into a general monstrosity, and is in no position to come in contact with the working class any more than the hand of a corpse can grip the hand of a live man. We raise the hammer of the workman to drive a final nail into the lid of this coffin of art."

DEMYAN BEDNY

In any discussion of the poetry of the masses in Russia one cannot overlook Demyan Bedny (Yefim Pridvorov; b. 1883). Though belonging to no group, he was regarded by all, until his recent decline, as preëminently the people's poet. He is the oldest poet of the revolution. His work had been published in Bolshevik periodicals even before the war, and in 1917 he did not have to be "converted," or to "accept" the revolution. He fitted right into it and remained its bard and champion through the years. If the institution of a poet laureateship existed in Soviet Russia, no one would contest Bedny's eligibility. Nearly all his verses were written for occasions, to order, at the demand of the country and the Party. Unconcerned about form, hardly sensitive to it, he has produced thousands of racy, conversational verses on current issues. He addressed the masses directly on problems of war and revolution and reconstruction; he gave them courage and confidence, entertained them with a bit of coarse humor, whetted their hatred and contempt for foreign and inner enemies, and kept them informed, stirred, exhorted, consoled. During the civil wars and the reconstruction period, Demyan Bedny's *agitki* (bits of agitation or propaganda) were the most direct and effectual means of governmental contact with the people. Their poetic value is small; few of those verses bear rereading, once their subject has become a matter of the past. But at the time of their publication they had a very great appeal; they were recited and sung by soldiers and workers, they penetrated the remote backwoods of Russia and the thick skulls of the peasants, whom no one could address more aptly than the man with the fetching pen name of Damian the Poor. Though a university graduate, Bedny is fond of referring to himself as a peasant, a *muzhik,* and he is, indeed, a master of the colorful folk speech, rich in parables, proverbs, unexpected phraseology and well-aimed epithets. He is at his best in his political fables, a *genre* that found considerable application under the old regime, when censorship conditions invited the use of the language of Aesop, La Fontaine, and the superb Russian fable writer, Ivan Krylov. Demyan Bedny gained his reputation by his prerevolutionary fables, in which he managed to dodge the censor with his nimble verses on birds, animals, inanimate objects, and simple rustics. The political message was perforce subtle, and the very form of fables demanded brevity and precision.

A perusal of Demyan Bedny's fables and less felicitous compositions gives one a broad idea of popular moods and issues in Russia during the years between the revolutions of 1905 and 1917, the civil wars, and reconstruction. It is extremely difficult to translate his vernacular, above all, his fables written in the Krylov lines of varying length. (Sir Bernard Pares, who admirably englished Krylov, might do justice to Demyan Bedny.) I can only offer an inadequate version of some bits about rustic Russia. The passionate desire for land on the part of half-starving peasants and the refusal of landowners to relinquish their holdings are frequently his theme. The following "fable" is named *Narodnik* ("A Lover of the People"), and depicts the agrarian phase in the elections for the Duma, in 1912:

> A landowner, on meeting a muzhik,
>   Foka, the Luckless,
> "Hey, Foka," he said, "you are famed as brainy,
>   Let us have a good chat,
>   While it's quiet here.
> Elections, you see, are close at the elbow.
> But a muzhik in politics, as you know,
>   Is a babe in the woods.
> Well, let us reason out: who should go to the Duma?
> I, for one, am ready. The heavy cross I will bear.
> Now you can vouch for me before the whole village:
> Our landowner, you may say, will go hand-in-glove with the
>   people.
> We might get together on almost everything.

Only forget all nonsense about land."
"Land!" Foka's mouth began to water.
"Land ... well, now ... a little land—no harm in that ...
    Some have too much, but as for us—oy, oy, how little ..."
"Ah, simpleton, what are you ranting about?
    To whom it has been given, has been given by God."
Moans Foka: "Ekh, if we too had ... just a little ...
    A chunk of land."
"My, my, Foka, how uncouth your brains,
    Rough bast!
Let us agree on the main points, and hang the trifles!"
    Here our Foka grew raging mad:
    "Hold on! What is this trifle you're wagging about?
You think you have found a fool?
Or have muzhiks ever seen any good from gentry?
    Think our memory is short?
Get to hell out of here, son of a dog, before
    We trim your hide!"

Half a dozen years later the "raging" mood of the peasants was
expressed less gently against the landowning class. Demyan Bedny
recorded this cumulative vindictiveness in his fable:

SAPLINGS

Five years ago, or thereabouts,
A certain landowner took a ride in the woods.
    On the coach box Filka lorded it,
    Such a stalwart, a regular hero!
"See, how it has grown up here! Used to be barren earth."
    The landowner admired the saplings.
"How about it, Filka? Fine young birches, what?
    That's where rods are growing! Suppose we get a bunch?
    To teach the muzhiks a lesson ... in case they're headstrong!"
"M-yes!" mooed Filka, slanting his eyes:
"M-yes ... as rods they're first-rate ...
    Fine saplings ... Birch rods ...
As they grow up, they'll make capital clubs!"

The moral of this little fable? Plain enough.
Years passed and passed—and the saplings grew up. (1918)

By 1930, the village was unrecognizable, what with the extermination of landowners and *kulaks,* voluntary or forced unfrocking of priests, and the turning of churches into clubs for collective farms (*kolhoz*). To that year belongs Demyan Bedny's jingly "Kolhoz Church," which shows incidentally a more outspoken and less subtle author:

> Dili-dili-dili-dong!
> What an income for pope Anton!
> Fat-bellied rich kulak
> Had not a care in his noddle.
> Sure it was a gainful toll:
> Dili-dili-dili-dong!
>
> Out was kicked pope Anton,
> Fat kulak curses his fate.
> In ex-church now for some time
> They've had a comyouth club, a movie,
> Where kids raise the devil:
> "We're kolhozers! Hip-hurrah!!"

The Bolshevik Revolution freed Bedny from the fetters of censorship and enabled him to unfold his power fully. It also robbed him of subtlety and of the *Beschränkung* that Goethe expected from a *Meister*. This, coupled with the rather indifferent and commonplace form of his verse, explains why, despite his unrivaled popularity and recognized services to the revolution (he has been decorated several times), Demyan Bedny is not the poet of the revolution in the sense that Mayakovsky is. Mayakovsky is rarely obvious, his verse does not settle down at once in the mind of the untrained reader but has to be reread, and read aloud, to be grasped. Once it penetrates one's consciousness, Mayakovsky's verse comes to stay; its original form and striking vocabulary help to make it unforgettable. Mayakovsky gave full expression to the nature of the revolution and its tempo, whereas Demyan Bedny performed the useful but ephemeral job of the journalist of the revolution, in verse. With the passing of the storm and stress, and the comparative normalization of life, Bedny threatens to become supernumerary. He continues to react to issues of the day, but his facile verse begins to sound monotonous and repetitious, and fails to answer the needs of an audience grown more exacting and critical. In recent years Bedny has been severely censured for his satirical treatment of everything pertaining to Russia before the revolution. A play of his, *The Ancient Heroes* (*Bogatyri*), in which he ridiculed the heroes of folklore and early history, and lampooned the conversion of the people to Christianity by the sainted Prince Vladimir (d. 1015; conversion, 988 or 989), was taken off the stage by the authorities; Tairov, director of the Kamerny (Chamber) Theater, was dismissed from his post for producing the play. This measure is characteristic of the present-day attitudes and conceptions in the Soviet Union, reflected in socialist realism, a theory of art which eschews wholesale condemnation of the past and demands of the writer a scientific treatment of the past in the light of the present. Bedny was reprimanded for his failure to credit the church with a definite contribution to national culture and for his levity with regard to such creations of the national mind as legendary and semilegendary heroes.

Demyan Bedny is now practically silent. His place is with the poets of the early phase of the revolution, when he played a temporarily dominant role as far as the mass audience was concerned. Though not a member of any of the contending groups, he belongs to the proletarian poets whom we are discussing in this chapter.

NEP—NOTES OF ALARM

Along with the braggadocio which had become routine in literary declarations, we begin to discern therein a note of alarm after the passing of the honeymoon of the revolution, that is, with the introduction of the NEP. There was, indeed, reason for alarm on the part of romantic revolutionists. For one thing, the partial reappearance of private enterprise, with all the concomitants of the personal profit motive, meant for them the end of revolutionary aspirations, the annulment of the fruits of heroic struggle and epochal victories against inner and foreign enemies. They failed to appreciate Lenin's idea of a "breathing spell," during which the conflict between private and social ownership would be reduced to the formula: Who will down whom? (*Kto kovo?*) They mourned and wept, gnashed their teeth, and fulminated against the "betrayal of October." Some plunged into Yeseninism, drowning their bewilderment in liquor and self-destruction; the proletarian poet Kuznetsov (1904–1924) killed himself. Others (Kirillov, Gerasimov), disgusted with the "Muscovite America," turned their backs on the new order and became its opponents. "Everydayness," a poem by Alexandrovsky, branded the drabness of the new life, "so mangy, so commonplace and absurd" as to make one feel "melancholy as a dog in nasty February weather," and tempt one "to smash one's head against the granite," in emulation of those "dreamers who depart from great work and duty." Even more gloomy and wrathful sounded Gerasimov, in his "Black Froth," a picture of NEP Moscow, in the grip of traders who "sell by the pound body and soul" and pollute life by cheap depravity. "What pain! What pain!" he exclaims as he watches the corruption of his ideal. From the gallery of a theater he observes the main floor, the "white lumps of sovbourgeois court ladies in shimmering silks," the uniformed and decorated sovdignitaries, and "grinding his teeth, blue-bloused and rude," he shouts to them:

> Bandage up your carmine lips,
> They are like ulcers—
> Vulgarly they ooze the past!
> Amid the crags of chairs and ribs
> My soul boils over with black foam.
> Smash the icicles of diamonds in your ears!
> Oh singers of toil, poets,
> And thou, sun,

. . .
Where art thou?
Strangle them with fiery braids,
Bright keen one,
Scorch them with thy red ore!
'Tis I, a blue-bloused union man,
Shouting from the gallery,
And who can drown my iron cry?

FELLOW TRAVELERS

Another immediate result of the NEP was the revival of the printed word, hitherto limited for the most part to official business and to thin booklets of verse. In 1921 there began to appear once more the traditional Russian "fat" monthlies which had played an important role for more than a century, serving both as a parliament of opinion (sufficiently veiled to pass the censor) and as a clearing-house for belles-lettres. Not only did communistic periodicals flourish, but even "neutral" and definitely unsympathetic reviews, such as *Khudozhestvennoie slovo, Rossia, Novaia Rossia, Sovremennik,* found sustainers and readers. A shower of stories and novels, mostly by young authors, flooded the parched market. Poetry, though well represented, was pushed to the background, where is has since remained. During the years of military communism the citizenry was exempt from paying for commodities and facilities; these were gratis, if there were any to be had. Under the NEP one had to pay for bread and transportation and theater tickets and printed matter. The NEP public was willing to pay— it was so much more normal and respectable to do so; but this public demanded its wares in abundance and variety, including melodrama and leg shows and agreeably shocking fiction. The demand created its supply.

This was more alarming than the pessimism and faintheartedness of the romantic revolutionists. The proletarian voice in literature was in danger of being drowned in an alien chorus. To be sure, the articulate enemies of the new order were few in number and could not be outspoken. Most of the new writers who displayed merit and attracted readers were known as "fellow travelers." Trotsky applied this name to authors who were somewhat in sympathy with the new order but failed to subscribe to it fully and to throw their lot on its side without reservations. "They do not grasp the revolution as a whole," wrote Trotsky, "and its communistic goal is foreign to them. . . . They are not the artists of the proletarian revolution, but its fellow travelers (*poputchiki*). . . . The question always comes up with regard to a fellow traveler: How far, up to what station is he going?" The term took root, and was used broadly and often arbitrarily; it was attached not only to Blok, Alexey Tolstoy, Ehrenburg (b. 1891), and Pilnyak (b. 1894), but even to Maxim Gorky. What treatment should be meted out to these authors by the proletarian state, became the most widely and most heatedly discussed question after 1921.

The official attitude, voiced in statements by the Central Committee of the Party and by its individual leaders, was one of cautious benevolence. The fellow travelers were regarded as a valuable asset which no state, let alone a culturally poor and backward state, could afford to squander. Time and again the Party gave instructions to treat the fellow travelers with tactful considerateness, to help them get adjusted to the new order, and perhaps to win them over eventually. Accordingly, these authors were readily published in state-controlled reviews and by state publishing houses. A. Voronsky, as editor of the new monthly, *Krasnaya nov'* ("Red Virgin Soil"), guided by his sense of literary values, allotted most of its pages to fiction written by fellow travelers. Opponents of his policy, however, accused him of a Trotskyist prejudice against proletarian writers.

These, or rather their spokesmen, were strongly opposed to the official policy. The "Smithy," for example, instructed its delegate to a government commission on proletarian culture to "protest against the unwise, utterly unwarranted, excessive attention bestowed on so-called literary 'spets' [specialists], [such as A. Tolstoy, Ehrenburg] and on the old [!] intelligentsia [such as Pilnyak, Nikitin (b. 1897), Shklovsky], whose importance is exaggerated because of an insufficient acquaintance with the output of proletarian writers." The "Smithy" insisted that the government assign to a central position the proletarian authors, and allot only the periphery to "fellow travelers, runts, abortions, and so on." More drastic were the demands of the group "October," and of its allies, "Young Guard," MAPP and RAPP. These demanded the hegemony of proletarian literature, which alone was to be entrusted with the "organization of the readers' psyche and consciousness" (note Bogdanov's phraseology) in the direction of a communistic society. The recrudescence of capitalistic tendencies under NEP conditions called for a strong proletarian cultural front to fight "the ideological onset of the bourgeoisie," the literature of "remnants of the gentry-bourgeois caste," and that of "petty bourgeois distorters of the revolution." The last epithet was meant for fellow travelers, who "reflected the revolution in a crooked mirror." These groups were opposed to any "peaceful coöperation" with nonproletarian tendencies in literature wherein "the laws of class struggle remain active." They demanded that proletarian writers show themselves as "good Bolsheviks," and maintain "ideological irreconcilability and intolerance."

THE "OCTOBER" GROUP AND ITS ALLIES

The "Smithy" was found wanting in its exercise of that Bolshevik slogan, and "October" was organized to counteract the softness of the "Blacksmiths." A bitter contest broke out between the two kindred groups, in which the "Smithy" was worsted, and finally wasted away, merging with the RAPP. The difference was not so much ideological as in regard to method and tempo, and was largely due to the composition of their membership. According to Lvov-Rogachevsky (1874–1930),[*] eighty per cent of the "Black-smiths" were workers, fifteen per cent peasants, and only five per cent intelligentsia. Eighty per cent of "October" were nonprole-tarian, but all of them were communists or young communists (*komsomol*), whereas only one-half of "Smithy" belonged to the Party. Further, while the "Octoberists" dated their ideas from October, 1917, most of the "Blacksmiths" had formed their out-look in prerevolutionary years, under the sweatshop conditions of the old industrial plants or in tsarist prison and exile.

It was a motley crowd that composed "October." There were a few workers in their midst, but most of them came from the ranks of nonproletarian "commoners"—the lower middle class, white-collar employes, peasants. Nearly all of them were young and militant, had been through the crucible of civil wars and their accompaniment—military communism—and were aflame with enthusiasm for building a new life under the aegis of the Party. They had no deep roots in the past; their burden of traditions was as light as their mental baggage, and they were bent on a for-ward march to sweep everything clean and conquer the world as they had recently vanquished the numerically superior and better-equipped armies of the White generals and the interventionists. They were buoyant and gay, defiant of obstacles, afraid of nothing. The NEP did not trouble them: they trusted the Party leadership and its wisdom, and were confident of their power to rise above the "black froth" of the temporarily revived bourgeoisie. Though half-baked and not purely proletarian, they were an unmistakable product of the October revolution.

A discussion of the prose literature, which regained its domi-nance after 1921, is outside the scope of this essay. A few words must be said here about the poetic expression of the "Octoberists." Their peculiar traits, outlined in the preceding paragraph, found a more direct and immediate reflection in lyrics and narrative poems

---

[*] *Ocherki proletarskoy literatury*, p. 179.

than in prose fiction. As one reads the poems of that period by Zharov (b. 1904), Doronin (b. 1900), Bezymensky, Utkin, Golodny, Svetlov (the last three b. 1903), and a score of others, one is aware of extreme youth, even adolescence, of the spirit of adventure and abandon, of amazing endurance and courage, and of fierce loyalty to the revolution and the Party. Though in form their verse is usually reminiscent of older poets, it is free from bookishness, from the mustiness of the study, for it was born directly out of life and its tempo. Alexander Zharov can compose a lyric in regular meter, as when he addresses the wind:

> You won't come, will you, you won't help me dress,
> When in fever I start shivering?
> But do you know—in my shoulder blade
> Yudenich is lodged, as a bullet?

And Zharov can shatter his lines and pound in a Mayakovsky staccato:

> Army of comyouths—
> Stands for: Up and go! . . . that's all!
> . . .
> Life . . .
> Why, how clear and simple:
> Up on your feet—and march!
> A whirlwind, comrades, a whirlwind!
> "Shoulder arms! Bayonets fixed!"
> From west, from north, from south—
> Poland,
> Denikin,
> Kolchak . . .
> Bivouac. Battle. Barracks.
> "March on in the morning!"

"Clear and simple" was the life of those youngsters, and they recalled it without ostentation or bravado. Nikolay Kuznetsov was one of the many who could reminisce of their heroic teens:

> Pal with them all and equal   I too marched with my rifle,
> (Cold shiver in my legs),   An urchin of fifteen.

Bezymensky.—The "Octoberists" lacked the pathos of the "Blacksmiths," their romantic glorification of the revolution, of labor and the factory. "The period of glorifying the revolution is being replaced by a period of showing the revolution in its reality, in its tangible manifestations," wrote Lelevich, an "Octoberist" poet and critic. During the NEP, communists were summoned to harness themselves to the prosaic tasks of economically rebuilding the devastated and demoralized land. It was hard to exchange the sword of adventure for the pick of the miner, and the music of the battlefield for the click of the counting board, but the "Octoberists" cheerfully submitted to this new phase of revolutionary discipline. Young A. Bezymensky chided the "cosmic-planetarian" "Blacksmiths," Yesenin and kindred writers of emotional lyrics about cows and dogs, as well as LEF preoccupation with "things-as-such":

> 'Tis nice to juggle
> Planets like balls!
> To chant electropoems to cosmos.
> But see if you can
> Discern the Dawn of the Future
> In some chairman or other
> Of a countytimbercommittee!
> 'Tis fine to sing
> To the revolution, as to a bride,
> Millions of hymns and ironpsalms,
> But do you know
> How, thanks to the Rubbertrust,
> We dug trenches
> Against our enemies?
> . . .
> Write hundreds of "Poems about Dogs,"
> But give us at least one
> About living man.
> Take any Labor-College Ted,
> Who is going to be
> Our tomorrow.

> Enough of heaven
> And the wisdom of things!
> Give us more of simple nails.
> Drop your heaven!
> Throw away your things!
> Give us the earth
> And living people!

Bezymensky has adequately voiced the spirit of his generation. In his epic songs, such as *Komsomolia,* and in his numerous lyrics, he has continued the note of Mayakovsky without Mayakovsky's futuristic trickery and his tragic inner conflict. Bezymensky is free from rifts and contradictions. He bubbles over with the joy of living under the Soviet flag. He is enraptured with the heroics of everyday life that offers so few material comforts but such a wealth of inspiration and assurance and faith in the future of man. He does not, like Gerasimov, fume and rage and grow disheartened at the sight of rich Nepmen when he encounters them in the theater. The contrast between the well-dressed bourgeoisie and his own shabbiness (for he shares with the masses the shortage of clothing and footwear) provokes his mild banter but fails to dampen his joviality:

> To the theater, like others, for a fee
> I came, but—it appears—I am different.
> I stroll in the lobby like a patch
> That sticks out of the velvets and silks.
>> In a rough linen blouse
>> (Not at all to show off)
>> I pass amid quick waves
>> Of flat lorgnetted eyes.
> I see: everyone, it seems,
> Who blocks my way,
> Has come up with a bottomless thirst
> To have a glimpse
> At . . . my felt boots.
>> Well, why not? They've no holes.
>> No mud is seen on them.

> Felt boots, of sheep's wool!
> Felt boots—shipshape!
> Poor shorn sheep,
> Your pride no one will understand.
> Unless it be the shoe
> Of that college student,
> That smiles with gaping mouth . . .
> . . . Away from the cozy easy-chairs,
> And down the stairs—head over heels.
> I step briskly and think gaily
> Of tomorrow's day in the factory—
> Of how my friend, my jolly workbench,
> Will laugh goodheartedly.
> And my felt boots in tune
> Stomp and crunch with gusto.
> Suddenly—causing embarrassed smiles—
> I went hippety-hop, clattering merrily:
> I caught up with
> Two redarmymen,
> (In felt boots!)
> With rifles,
> Discussing a book
> By Lenin.

Bigotry—RAPP—At the Post.—The "October" output (I speak here of poetry only) will remain an interesting record of the revolutionary youth in the days of storm and stress and early recovery. But the literary productions of that group were one thing and the declarations of its spokesmen another. The latter had their center in the periodical *Na postu* ("At the Post"), in which they carried on a vehement campaign in the name of "October," and the allied "Young Guard," MAPP and VAPP. In passing, one may mention the nonproletarian origin and affiliations of the most fanatical Atpostists, such as Rodov (b. 1893), Lelevich (b. 1901), Averbach (b. 1903).

At the Post undertook to champion the most extreme views of proletcult, from which it differed only in one essential point—

one of strategy rather than principle: whereas the Bogdanovites desired autonomy for proletcult, independence from the government and the Party, the Atpostists hankered for government and Party recognition and sanction, for an official stamp of approval of their leadership and control in literary matters. The latter group lacked the erudition and broad culture of Bogdanov, but they made up for that by aggressiveness, bigotry, and uncompromising hostility toward all those who were not with them. The promising beginnings of proletarian authorship were inflated by *At the Post* to exaggerated proportions in order to justify the contention that a proletarian literature was already in existence and that all other literature was unnecessary and even dangerous in a workers' state. The group waged a bitter war against Voronsky and the "Defile" group, who welcomed fellow travelers in the belief that not only were these superior artists, but that, on the whole, they correctly reflected the revolution. Though not communists, the fellow travelers were loyal to the new order, and a large number of them had fought on its behalf during the civil wars. *At the Post* denied the fellow travelers any chance for proving useful or loyal, since they were hopelessly bourgeois or petty-bourgeois, and therefore could but distort the revolution instead of reflecting it. The title of "counterrevolutionary" was lavishly bestowed on writers of other groups (A. Tolstoy, Ehrenburg, Pilnyak), while those who met the prerequisites were just as generously praised to the skies. At the same time *At the Post* approved the alliance of the proletarian groups with such decidedly nonproletarian groups as the Union of Peasant Writers, LEF, and the constructivists. This was obviously a strategic move to win supremacy over the fellow travelers by organization, since they could not attain it by superior talent.

At the Literary Post.—The policy of *At the Post* threatened to disrupt literary activity by sowing discord and suspicion, by showering flattery and undeserved praise on unripe talent, and by disparaging and throwing mud at gifted fellow travelers. By sharply classifying editors and critics as "loyalists" and "capitulants," the group created an unhealthy atmosphere of hostility, unscrupulous politics, and discouragement to those who wanted only to create and to keep out of brawls. The Party declared itself repeatedly against "narrow cliquishness" and these "extremely abnormal interrelations of writers' groups, circles, and alliances." Official resolutions of the Central Committee rebuked all efforts at a "hegemony of proletarian writers," and reiterated the demand for a "tactful and heedful" treatment of fellow travelers. In 1925 *At the Post* was forced to suspend publication; but early in 1926 it came out under a new name, *Na literaturnom postu* ("At the Literary Post"), with a promise to adhere to broad literary lines and not to meddle in issues of "narrow organization." The Atlitpostists soon proved, however, even more intolerant and unscrupulous than the Atpostists. The new editor, Averbach, proclaimed a slogan: "Ally or enemy!" No neutral position was suffered; either one agreed with Averbach's group, or one was denounced as an enemy of the Soviets. Posing as the only orthodox Marxian organ, *At the Literary Post* demanded that every writer apply *diamat* (dialectical materialism) to his productions. It flaunted such loud slogans as "bolshevization of literature" and "a five-year plan of literature." A vulgarized sociological criticism was introduced, with a rigid "class" yardstick that was applied both to former and to contemporary authors, resulting in the final verdict of ally or enemy. These "critics" enthroned favorites, most of whom were swept to the rubbish heap of nonentities after the collapse of RAPP, and, on the other hand, they endeavored to destroy those in disfavor, be it Furmanov (1891–1926) (author of *Chapayev*), Sholokhov (b. 1905) (*Quiet Don*), or Mayakovsky. There is hardly any question about the partial responsibility of *At the Literary Post* for the suicide of Mayakovsky. It persecuted the poet without abatement even after he joined, presumably in self-defense, the RAPP; in fact, even after his death. In brief, literature was terrorized.

Two reasons may be given for the persistence of this group in the face of opposition on the part of leading authors and in defiance of official condemnation of its brand of policy. For one thing, they were shrewd politicians, knowing how to pull strings within the Party and how to increase their power by means of alliances with other easily dominated groups, and by questionable means of swelling their own membership. Thus the RAPP issued a call for "shock workers" to fill the literary ranks, relying on the docility of culturally immature factory hands whom the Averbach gang could hold as a whip over recalcitrant members. In the second place, one must recall the grave inner conflicts within the Communist Party during the nineteen-twenties, especially after the death of Lenin. The government was anxious to preserve the "general line" against threatening deviations to the right and the left. The Atpostists and Atlitpostists made use of the psychological moment for their vociferous clamor against non-Party elements. Their heresy hunt assumed the coloration of anti-Trotskyism at one moment, and of anti-any-opposition at another. However critical of this group, the government regarded it as a lesser evil, and while it suspended various organizations suspected of Trotskyism and other oppositional tendencies, it suffered the RAPP as a wartime nuisance. The inauguration of the first Five-Year Plan, at the end of the 'twenties, demanded an even stricter policy against all tendencies that might imperil the success of the gigantic undertaking. *At the Literary Post* mixed its inquisitorial literary campaign with outcries against *kulaks* and doubting Thomases who dared question the feasibility of the Plan.

1932—End of RAPP.—It was dangerous, if not suicidal, to oppose RAPP and its organ during those years of nervous strain, unless one's courage was coupled with a position beyond the reach of the Averbachs. Demyan Bedny had the temerity to dissociate himself publicly from the Atlitpostists, in 1926, after having served the cause of proletarian culture for years, long before the inception of proletcult. More outspoken in his opposition to the RAPP was Maxim Gorky, whose life was a fight against tyranny of any kind. Upon his final return to the Soviet Union, in 1928, Gorky plunged into a many-faceted cultural activity which consumed, literally, the last eight years of his life. He was particularly concerned about the education and professional training of young writers, and here he collided with the corrupting influence of RAPP. Without mincing words, Gorky attacked the boastful and dictatorial claims of the Atlitpost clique. These claims, he wrote (prophetically, in the light of subsequent revelations), "very often emanate from amidst the parasites of the new master of our land—the working class, from persons who have not betrayed us as yet, but who may betray us at any moment." In the wake of Gorky there appeared an editorial in *Pravda* against "cliquism" in the RAPP.

In April, 1932, the resolution of the Central Committee of the Party disbanded the RAPP and other literary groups and organizations, once and for all. With the completion of the first Five-Year Plan, with the advent of a sense of comparative security on inner and foreign fronts, the government and the Party felt the situation firm enough to dispense with the policy of class war in the literary field. Averbach and his clique were clipped of their power and gradually ousted from all positions of trust and responsibility. Gorky lent his aid and guidance to the organization of the first Union of Soviet Writers, which has since remained the only professional literary organization. The sole political creed required of a qualified member of the union is loyalty to the Soviet regime. As to literary theories, socialist realism has been accepted as the most suitable direction for the period. Broadly interpreted, this theory is a direct continuation of Russian realism, minus its negativism and plus the vision of a socialized commonwealth in the making. In 1932 the atmosphere was cleansed, and the writers have been able to breathe more freely and to create without fear of petty persecution.

The proletcult and its derivatives, down to RAPP, performed effective service by bringing to the fore and clarifying many issues, and driving away actual enemies of the new order. Their main service, however, was a negative one: they demonstrated the danger and the futility of trying to control and guide creative effort by browbeating methods. The Party had faced a difficult task. For nearly two decades it watched over the literary battles, endeavoring to bring about a painless solution. While definitely partial to proletarian authors and anxious to raise their number and stature, the Party was reluctant to spoil the child by excessive petting. Hence the "protectorate" over nonproletarian authors and the tactful methods employed to win their loyalty.

Chapter VI ⌁ A Glance at the Recent Scene

IN THE LAST decade, poetry has entered a "normal" phase in the development of Soviet letters—normal in the sense of its being subordinated to prose in influence and output; normal, too, in its having outlived formalistic vagaries and eccentricities, and having started on a wide synthetic road wherein merge divergent paths and byways. The average Soviet poet today is a masterly craftsman who has at his disposal a variety of form and meter, an unhackneyed vocabularly, and novel images. The years of theoretical battles, of outlandish experiments and extremes, have not been altogether in vain: the younger poets have fallen heirs to a vast, chaotically plowed-up field, and they have profited from the findings and errors of their forerunners. Similarly, in regard to its content, present-day Soviet poetry is as free from the raw solipsism of early futurists and imagists as it is from the blatant cosmism and iron panegyrics of the "Blacksmiths" and the soap-box *agitki* of many of the "Octoberists." The Soviet poet no longer feels duty-bound to glorify the tractor when his heart goes out to the flaxen-haired girl. Emotional lyrics, purely descriptive poetry, and songs of patriotism and enthusiasm for the new life commingle and usually sound natural and sincere. The growing vogue for narrative poems and epics of past and present events is another indication that the poise and calm of peaceful reconstruction have replaced the turbulence of destructive war and revolution. Toward the end of the 1930's the aggressiveness of the Axis powers became a menace to Soviet frontiers in Europe and Asia, and it was echoed in a new wave of militant verse. No longer romantic, blatant, and bellicose, as civil-war poetry had been, the later prewar verse spoke of the threatening enemies with calm dignity, in tones of confidence in the ultimate triumph of the arms and ideas of the socialist state.

LYRIC POETRY

Lyric poetry has undergone some marked changes since 1917. The early stage of abstract cosmism and psalms to iron and concrete gave way to more specific motives by such pupils of Mayakovsky as Bezymensky, Zharov, and others. These were mostly of the Soviet youth, who had fought in the civil wars and were full of enthusiastic loyalty to the Party and of cocky confidence in themselves and in the proletariat that had just come out victorious over the armed forces of the capitalistic world. Bezymensky was the spokesman for the ascetic youth who had nothing but contempt for conventional human feelings and passions. He had no sympathy for his reactionary father, and only scornful pity for his mother who tried to deprive him of his Party ticket, failing to realize that he "bore the Partticket not in his pocket but in his very self." In another poem Bezymensky expressed the indifference of his generation to spring, its color and stimulus, for their vital concern is about "the prime cost of Soviet commodities." Girls? Love?

> There are some who are anxious for girls' lips.
> As for me, I worry about factory stacks.

The Bezymensky phase was too artificial, too much of the head, to last long. (Bezymensky himself has since broadened his range and approach.) Lyric poetry was released from its fetters by another group of youthful poets, who had also been at various fronts and were likewise faithful to the Party, but who refused to "tread on the throat of their song" as Mayakovsky and some of his followers endeavored to do. Life and youth claimed their rights. After years of horror and bloodshed, of unbelievable privations and suffering, the survivors, the young survivors especially, pounced greedily upon the things they had been denied—upon things in the literal

sense, objects of the surrounding world. Like Selvinsky, these poets
reveled in the description of tangible matter, of food and trees, of
the thousand-and-one items one encounters every day in normal
life, which to them had the wonder of the unseen or of the almost
forgotten. "Bitter mustard whets one's appetite for meat," sang one
of these (Utkin). There was in their lyrics the pagan joy of giving
vent to one's five senses.

Next to the fascination of tangible things, they rediscovered
the world of emotions, which had been suppressed and tabooed
by the overpuritanical comyouths. These were no longer ashamed
to show sympathy for uncongenial parents, to cite one example.
Unlike Bezymensky, Yosif Utkin in his "Song of My Mother"
speaks tenderly of the woman whose son comes on a visit from the
front and finds her bewildered by the clash of revolution and tradition. There is no scorn in the questions he asks with her:

> Ah, poor mother,
> Ah, dear mother,
> Whom are we to love?
> Whom to condemn?

Unafraid of tenderness is another of these lyricists, Mikhail
Golodny. While fighting at the front, he visualizes his homecom-
ing, and here too the mother motif sounds unsuppressed:

> Mother will spurt salty pain,
> And bending over her bed
> Long I shall not untangle
> Her bony embrace.
> When we two remain alone,
> I'll lock myself in heavy silence.
> As she will ask about the war,
> Her voice will stop short in tremor.
> I shall toss her a lie—
> Is it for me
> To tell her of the war?

Most of these poets were youngsters when called to action. Their thoughts and feelings were formed under the sign of war, and bore its stamp. On sleepless nights, the rain pattering on the roof, the poet (Golodny) tosses and reflects, "war casting its huge shadow on the bed," and his muse appropriately arrayed:

> One wing shattered,
> Rifle on her shoulder.

Small wonder if this muse inspires the poet to subdue personal motives and to sound the alarm:

> Arise! A dozen countries are in arms,
> The challenge already is hurled at us.
> Look: my faithful drum
> Is split in two ...
> Arise! Summon your comrades.
> Budenny[1] is at the gate.
> Your poem of love
> Shall not be finished this year.

With the termination of battles and alarms, love songs were resumed, but even in the war songs one often hears the gaiety of carefree youth that dances unto death with "a white-toothed smile":

> Marches with white-toothed smile
> Drummer youthful.
> Dance the horses.
> Trumpets pour
> Bright brass waters.
> Horses keep time to
> Swelling veins.
> Trumpeters thunder a quadrille,
> Flakes of foam settle down
> Fluttering dust.
>
> (Utkin)

Contemplative admiration of the objective world and preoccupation with emotional experiences are apt to drive a poet into the

---

[1] A Red cavalry general (b. 1883).

bog of individualism or even egotism. Soviet society cannot afford
such unsocial, self-centered currents as symbolism or futurism.
But the poets here discussed are immunized against this danger,
for they have drunk deep of the revolution, they have been bap-
tized in its fire and blood. The personal and social motifs in
their lyrics commingle and blend without effort. Unhesitatingly
and spontaneously they subordinate the personal to the social, for
to them the social ideal is not an acquired external but the very
essence of their life, for which they have lived and fought. Echoing
the early "iron" motive of the revolution, young Utkin proclaims
the monism of his cause:

> All!
> Even the tenderness of singing songs—
> All!
> And even the body's tenderness—
> For the iron blossoming,
> For the only cause!

Yet devotion to the "cause" does not exclude responsiveness to
voices of nature. With the conceit of youth, Utkin pats himself
on the back as he boasts of combining the soldier of the revolution
and the lyrical poet:

> How glad I am
> To emerge into the plans of peace
> Equally sustaining
> The valor of a citizen
> And the lyrics of woman's hair.

A similar combination of notes sounds in most of the latest
Soviet lyrics, in those of M. Svetlov, V. Lugovskoy (b. 1901), V.
Gusev (b. 1909), P. Antokolsky (b. 1896), and a host of others.
Healthy and optimistic, proud builders of a new life, and passionate
affirmers of life as such, with its joys and struggles, the young poets
sing naturally, *comme les oiseaux,* of themselves and of the collective force that gives meaning to their efforts. M. Golodny may

sound bombastic, but he voices the conviction of his fellow poets
when he says:

> With cascades of bronze symphonies
> I have come to awaken our youth.
> And having touched the mystery of cosmos,
> We're aflame, we're aflame, all of us together,
> Our millionfold head directed
> At the silent infinity of days.

These lyricists, it should be noted, differ from the Mayakovsky-
Bezymensky group also in favoring regular meter; most of their
verses are in iambics or trochees.

SONGS

Russia has always been a singing country, the song often serving
as the only outlet for the untutored and oppressed masses. In recent
years the popular demand for new songs expressive of contemporary themes has prompted a good many poets to compose both
modern "romances" and verses in the style of folk songs. The in-
tensive translation of the literature and folklore of national minorities, stimulated by the official Soviet policy, has further enhanced
the spread of the song *genre*. Unlike other forms of poetry, the
success or failure of a song is conclusively proved by its popular
acceptance or rejection, allowing of course for the contributory role
of its musical composer. Young poets like V. Gusev, S. Mikhalkov,
A. Surkov (b. 1899), and particularly V. Lebedev-Kumach (b. 1898),
have eclipsed other and better poets in the measure of acclaim they
have received for their songs. The extremely critical attitude of
Soviet audiences, and their growing sense of discrimination, may
serve as some assurance that the popularity of a song is not meas-
ured by cheapness or a low standard. Such a song, once it hits the
mark, is caught up by millions of Soviet citizens by way of the
screen, the radio, the platform, the printed page, and becomes part
and parcel of the folk repertory. As a sample of these songs one
may cite the "Song of the Motherland" composed for the film

Circus by Lebedev-Kumach, typical in its simplicity and in the patriotic sentiment that has grown intense in the land. Here is an almost literal translation of this song:

(*Refrain:*) Vast is my native land.
Has many forests, fields, rivers.
I know of no other country
Where man breathes so freely.

From Moscow to the very borderlands,
From the southern mountains to the seas of the north,
Man goes up and down as master
Of his immense motherland.
(*Refrain*)

A spring breeze wafts across our land.
Day by day it gets merrier to live,
And no one in the world knows how
To laugh better, and to love.
(*Refrain*)

But severely we shall knit our brows,
Should an enemy design to break us.
Like a bride we love our motherland,
We guard her like a tender mother.
(*Refrain*)

All over our land, life freely and broadly
Flows, like opulent Volga.
For youth all roads are open here,
Full respect for old folks.
(*Refrain*)

Our fields no eye can embrace,
You cannot recall all our cities.
Our proud word "tovarishch"
Of all fair words is dearest to us.
(*Refrain*)

With this word we are at home ev'rywhere—
No blacks, no colored folks for us.
This word is familiar to all,
It finds us near ones far and wide.
(*Refrain*)

After the adoption of the 1936 Constitution, Lebedev-Kumach
added these verses:

> At our table ev'ryone feels welcome,
> Each rewarded for his merits.[2]
> With golden letters we have written
> The Stalinite people's law.
> (*Refrain*)
> The grandeur and glory of these words
> No years whatever shall erase:
> Man always has the right
> To education, rest, and work.[3]
> (*Refrain*)

BALLADS

Closely allied to the song is the ballad, which has grown popular both in recitation and song. The prevailing theme is personal
and mass heroism in the revolution, the civil wars, and the reconstruction period. Typical of such a ballad song is M. Svetlov's
"Grenada," which took the country as by storm. It is one of Svetlov's civil-war pieces, written before the recent conflict in Spain.
The appeal of "Grenada" [*sic*] is due to such of its balladic merits
as fantasy and grim humor, coupled with an ingenuous inter-
nationalism.

GRENADA

We rode at a trot,
We sped into battle,
The song "Little Apple"
Held in our teeth.
Ah, this little song
Hovers to this day
Over the young grass,
The steppe's malachite.

But a different song,
Of a faraway land,
My buddy carried
Along on his saddle.
He sang, glancing all the while
At his native fields:
"Grenada, Grenada,
Grenada of mine!"

---

[2] Reference to Clauses 12, 121, 119, 118, of the Constitution. The communist aspiration—from each according to his ability, to each according to his need—is toned down
to the socialist maxim: to each according to his merit.

[3] See the preceding note.

This little song
He has learned by heart.
How came Spain's melancholy
To this Ukrainian?
Answer, Alexandrovsk,
And Kharkov, reply:
Since when have you begun
In Spanish to sing?
Tell me, O Ukraine:
Does not 'mid your corn
Lie the shaggy cap
Of Taras Shevchenko?[4]
Wherefrom, my buddy,
Comes your song:
"Grenada, Grenada,
Grenada of mine!"

He is slow in answer,
The dreamy Ukrainian:
"Little brother, Grenada
I found in a book.
A pretty name,
A high honor.
In Spain there is
A Grenada county.
I left my hut,
I went to war,
The Grenada land
For to give the peasants.
Farewell, my dear ones,
Farewell, my kinsmen.
Grenada, Grenada,
Grenada of mine!"

On we sped, dreaming
Of mastering quickly
The grammar of battle,
The battery language.
The sun now rose,
Now set again,
My horse grew tired
Galloping the steppes.
The squadron played
The song "Little Apple"
With bows of suffering
On violins of time.
But where, O my buddy,
Is that song of yours:
"Grenada, Grenada,
Grenada of mine!"

His pierced body
Slid down to the earth.
For the first time my comrade
Has left the saddle.
I beheld: over the corpse
The moon bent down,
The dead lips breathed: "Grena ..."
Yes! To a faraway land,
To a reach beyond the clouds,
Has gone my buddy,
And taken along his song.
Since then his native fields
Have no longer heard:
"Grenada, Grenada,
Grenada of mine!"

The squadron failed to note
The loss of one warrior,
And the song "Little Apple"
They sang to the end.
Only 'cross the sky softly

---

[4] A celebrated Ukrainian poet. See p. 87.

Crept, after a bit,
A tearlet of rain.
New songs
Life invents.
Let us not, buddies,
Mourn for songs.
Let us not, let us not,
Let us not, my friends ...
Grenada, Grenada,
Grenada of mine!

FOLK MOTIFS

It is only natural that, with the rise of the masses and their prestige in national life, folk motifs should assume a growing dominance in Soviet arts. Their presence in literary expression is quite notable, both in illiterate folk productions and in written poetry. The keynote, in the latter, was struck by the October revolution. In its most significant record, *The Twelve,* Alexander Blok intercalated passages reminiscent of the *chastushka* swing and tone. The *chastushka* is primarily a village jingle anonymously composed by local wits on some current topic, the pattern, epithets, and tune remaining traditional, with slight variations. Demyan Bedny owed his popularity in large measure to his *chastushka*-like ditties that spread like wildfire during the civil wars and were sung by soldiers and civilians. Even Mayakovsky, an urban poet if there ever was one, made abundant use of the *chastushka* rhythm and vocabulary, especially in his journalistic verses and placards. The ancient Russian sagas, the *byliny,* and other forms of folklore including song, fairy tale, ritual verse, have fed the Soviet muse in ever-increasing doses. For illustration one must turn again to Demyan Bedny, who borrowed lavishly from the folk treasury for his fables, lyrics, long narratives, and plays. A number of younger poets have followed in this direction. Among them, Alexander Prokofyev has been particularly apt in employing folklore motifs and methods in his poems of the civil wars and of the present-day village. Prokofyev occasionally exemplifies in Soviet poetry the too-zealous folklorists whose overstylization borders on the ludicrous. Maxim Gorky chided him for applying to his characters such stock hyperboles as

> His mustaches were reins,
> His beard, a harrow.

Kirsanov.—One offshoot of this movement toward folk poetry may be seen in the fantasies of the gifted young poet, S. Kirsanov (b. 1906). In his more than a dozen books he has shown a continuous growth and expansion. For a time, as a pupil of Mayakovsky, he was infatuated with formalistic tricks, producing verbal and syntactic oddities, his aspiration being

> To plunge from the cliff of metaphors to the bottom—
> A diver after the pearls of words.

That early period served him as good training in mastering the intricacies of language, meter, rhythm, and sound. To this time belongs his translation of Verlaine's *Chanson d'automne,* which in musical perfection and closeness to the spirit of the original eclipsed the numerous preceding versions. Omitting his subsequent phases, I shall mention only his latest, the fabrication of a new species of fairy tales.

There was a time when Soviet pedagogues frowned upon fairy tales as an opiate for the tender minds of children, breeding non-materialistic notions and superstitions. The huge success of Korney Chukovsky's *Crocodile* and similar nonsense verses by him and by Zhitkov (1876–1938), Marshak (b. 1887), and other brilliant poets for children, and of the more recent tales by Kirsanov, indicates the passing of that phobia, along with other symptoms of what Lenin dubbed "leftist infantilism." In his tales Kirsanov makes good use of his technical skill, blending the fantastic element with social problems of our day. Like all good children's literature, his tales make fascinating reading for adults; indeed, designed for children, they surpass Kirsanov's earlier, largely formalistic efforts by their clarity and by the easy flow which Kirsanov imparts to his verse despite its endless variety of meter and rhythm. His neologisms, hybrid words, onomatopes, and other oddities have the graceful naturalness of nursery rhymes, and neatly fit the subject. Though composed after the traditional model of fairy tales, Kirsanov's narratives thrill the reader by the abundant technical terms sprinkled through them, and by their frequent references to contemporary issues.

Kirsanov's finest success is his *Cinderella* (*Zolushka*). A masterpiece in form and plot, it may rank with *Alice in Wonderland;* there is more social pathos in its humor, however, than in its English counterpart. The subtitle is "A Poem of All Fairy Tales"; it contains, indeed, episodes from world-wide fairy tales, such as those of the magic carpet and Red Riding Hood, or such Slavic themes as Deathless Kashchey from the Firebird cycle. Kirsanov enhances the fun by placing the plot in our own time, mingling the supernatural with telephone and radio, and alternating anthropomorphic devices with such realistic scenes as that of Cinderella's sisters preening themselves for the ball with the aid of up-to-date cosmetics. Kirsanov's deviation from the Grimms' version appears at the outset when the sisters daydream of a prince "with a million to his bank account." On the family's return from the ball, the father, who has had too much to eat, suffers from an attack of hiccoughs; he unbuttons his waistcoat, and clamors for his favorite pill, "Dr. Julius' gilded pill." Cinderella is driven to town for the pill, and here begin her adventures in the snow-buried forest, and later in the city. Kirsanov boldly mixes fantastic items from universal tales, here and there giving them a modern slant, skipping from archaisms to the latest technological cry, or to a village *chastushka*. To translate Kirsanov adequately, one must possess the

gift of a Lewis Carroll. I can only offer a sample passage, stripped
unfortunately of its bewitching rhythm and rhyme:

> Out on the road steps Cinderella—
> She calls the ducks, the ducks comply.
> Sparrows screech in German: *zurück!*
> And share their paltry finds.
> Stradivarius-like writhes the cat,
> Washes his face for politeness' sake,
> And perching on the back-window ledge
> Up he strikes a grand purrucchio. . . .

Kirsanov varies his meter and tone according to the moods he
suggests, humor or satire, sadness or joy. When the narrative
touches on Cinderella's misery, her toil and vicissitudes, especially
the wintry night in the dark forest, the bantering tone changes to
a highly emotional one. Here we have an epitomic presentation of
man's economic slavery. The poem is interspersed with social implications, but without offensive obviousness: Kirsanov is an artist.
With pathetic humor he describes the toys and luxuries in the shop
windows, eager to fall into the frozen little hands of Cinderella,
who gazes at them longingly from the street. Kirsanov emphasizes
the original motif of this ancient tale, the motif of have-nots
versus haves. The poem ends on a major note, in an apotheosis of
Cinderella amidst marvels and stunts, from the oldest conceptions
of human imagination to dropping parachutes and somersaulting
planes.

Tvardovsky.—A curious mixture of epic and fairy tale may be
found in A. Tvardovsky's *Muravia Land*. The author knows intimately the village, its speech and lore, and its problems. Like his
two previous poems of Soviet peasantry, this one, his best, though
saturated with village atmosphere, differs significantly from Soviet
rustic poetry. Tvardovsky's peasant is free from the burlesquerie
one finds in Demyan Bedny, nor is he endowed with the mystic
sweetness and otherworldliness of Klyuyev and Yesenin. He faintly

resembles Nekrasov's peasant, minus the halo the "penitent nobles" bestowed upon their victims, the gadflies of their conscience.

Muravia Land abounds in folkloristic features such as legend, superstition, ritual song and dance, sayings and proverbs. But these do not protrude as superimposed ornamentation; adroitly they are woven into the body of the poem and appear inseparable from its pattern. What prevents these traditional forms from sounding remote and frozen is the mass of modern concepts and terms poured into them—the radio, the tractor, the collective farm, the Soviet. The *chastushka,* for example, an old and familiar form, Tvardovsky uses for themes suggesting the radical change that has taken place in village conditions. This is illustrated in the festivities which occur early in the poem and toward the end. On both occasions Tvardovsky mingles the old and the new with skill and social insight. In the first, village *kulaks* carouse and swill vodka in memory of those of their kind who have been dispossessed and exiled. They shout and drink and weep with abandon, in full knowledge of their doom as a class. From the frankness of their loosened tongues we learn of their sense of self-importance as opulent farmers, as well as of their undercover machinations against the government collectors of grain. One of them, presumably the host, strikes up a song, old in words and tune, but quite timely in its allegoric application to the oppressive new order:

> "Wherefore, God's birdie,
>   Dost not peck grain seeds?
>   Wherefore, tiny one,
>   Dost not sing loud songs?"
>
> Little bird answers:
> "Life in a cage I relish not.
>   Throw open my prison cell,
>   Into the free I will fly."

More elaborate is the description of a wedding feast on a collective farm, as the story draws to an end. An abundant harvest has been gathered, a red flag waves over the bride's hut, and the revelers are gay and free from care and worry. We witness the seemingly immutable conservatism of peasant customs and conventions in their wedding ceremonies, their dances, songs, drinking toasts. Here is the old mother recalling her own joyless youth, at the time when wife beating was accepted as a sign of respectability, to be expected by every bride. She sings a traditional lament, with references to the little swallow that must fly to foreign lands, and to the orphaned maiden going off to a home of strangers. Traditionally, the bride is here expected to shed floods of tears, but the young people of the present-day village refuse to weep for what is past and gone. Tvardovsky gives expression to the cheerfulness of the new village in a superb passage, describing a folk dance to the music of an accordion, the rhythm fittingly reflecting the sounds and movements. As is customary, the music and dance alternate with a song (or are accompanied by one). A common *chastushka* is given here, with the words slightly changed to give it a new twist, marking the modernization of Holy Russia:

> Out steps an impish girl—
> Make way, dancing choir!
> Her new white skirt
> She plucks with two fingers:

> "They've tried to marry me off,
> Talk me into it they've failed.
> I don't want to leave the commune,
> Not even for marriage's sake.

> 'What sort of lad are you?'
> I'll ask the lad.
> 'You're a lad all right, but not a flier.
> As for me, I want a flier.' "

The burden of the poem is the ancient theme of a man setting out in quest of the Promised Land. Nikita Morgunok, unwilling to join the collective farm, harnesses his horse and leaves the village to journey toward the legendary Muravia Land. Morgunok is neither a *kulak* nor a pauper, but of the category made much of by Lenin—a *serednyak,* a "middler," that is, a peasant just above the point of starvation. Morgunok clings to his puny but private property with the tenacity of a hereditary husbandman. Tvardovsky shows both sympathy and understanding in his portraiture of this vanishing species, the individual landholder in the Soviet Union. One must realize the difficulty for a young Soviet poet, born into the new order, of depicting attachment to property without rancor and mockery. Morgunok is rendered decidedly likable in his love for the soil and its gifts, even for the arduous toil it entails. The poetization of the sinful feeling of proprietorship is particularly apt in the description of Morgunok's devotion to his horse, an animal of rather indifferent points but of remarkable intuition and wisdom; in fact, it is the horse alone with whom its master takes counsel on the eve of his departure for Muravia Land. Soviet readers are introduced to a proprietor whose passion for ownership emanates, not from greed for acquisition or exploitation, but from an inherent love for earth and beast; such a passion they may condemn as old-fashioned, yet not as vicious. It is this passion, however, that impels Morgunok to flee from the collective: he does not trust his beloved soil, his friendly horse, to an impersonal organization that regiments the individual farmer. His ideas and ideals are those of a petty proprietor, a "rugged individualist," as is evident from his conception of the Promised Land:

> Muravia the ancient, Muravia Land.
> Far and wide, from side to side,
> The land is your own, all round.
> Plant, if you will, just one seed—
> But then, it's your own.
> Don't have to ask anybody,
> Yourself alone you heed.
> Going to reap? Reap away!
> Going for a drive? Drive away!

> All you see before you is your own,
> Just stroll about and spit at ease.
> The well is yours, the firs are yours,
> Even to all the fir cones.
> All year long, both summer and winter,
> Ducks dive in the lake.
> And, God save the mark,
> There is no *kommunia* nor *kolkhozia*.[5]
> To all peasant rules and customs
> Muravia is faithful.
> Muravia, Muravia—
> A jolly fine land!

Like millions of other prerevolutionary peasants throughout vast Russia, Morgunok is "in the grip of the soil," to use the phrase of Gleb Uspensky (1840–1902). He dreams of unmolested private ownership as the peak of happiness, his ideal exemplar being the local *kulak,* Ilya Bugrov, wealthy shopkeeper and hoarder of grain on the sly. If he could only rise to Bugrov's level, to be in a position to exchange greetings with him as with an equal, to have the honor of entertaining him in his hut,

> To chew the rag on this and that,
> To hum a song with half-closed eyes,
> Then arm in arm, the two of them,
> To stroll for a look at the fields of grain.

Such is Nikita Morgunok, a typical *seredynak.* Tvardovsky's task is to bring him to the collective farm, by convincing him, empirically, of its superiority over individual landholding. This is a gradual process, as it has been with millions of Morgunoks. Our Morgunok's Odyssey proves instructive; it cures him of many superstitions and of his credulity, and, in the end, of the Muravia utopia. Cheated and robbed of his beloved horse by the fugitive former *kulak* Bugrov, in return for Morgunok's friendship and road hospitality, the gullible *muzhik* suffers his first disillusionment. Searching for his horse, he looks into a settlement of Gypsies,

---

[5] Commune; collective farm.

traditional horsethieves. To his amazement, even the Gypsies have changed their ways and are living a happy, settled life on a model collective farm. Morgunok's prejudices are strong enough to keep him from accepting the proffered Gypsy hospitality. He is unaware of the fact that in Soviet Russia the Gypsies, like other "inferior" nationalities, have proved their right to economic and cultural equality and have their own schools, newspapers, and even opera house, where they perform Mérimée-Bizet's *Carmen* and Pushkin-Rachmaninov's (1873–1943) *Gypsies* in their native language.

He wanders on, and comes upon a village of individual farmers. Here he expects to find an adumbration of Muravia. What he sees there, however, is poverty and stagnation. Half-starved peasants loiter about, whittle, scratch their heads, and philosophize on the advantages of their good old system. But the women refuse to see with their men's eyes. One of them draws a graphic comparison between their "individualistic" life and that on the collective farm, branding her kind "unpeople" as against the collectivist "people-people":

> "Lo, I go about with empty breasts—
> Such a fine life, forsooth!
> With people-people, wheat
> Is bending in the breeze,
> But with unpeople, straw
> Wallows over the court.
> With people-people, children
> All day frolic in playgrounds,
> By a common table in a row
> Sit like turtledoves.
> While mine live in this world
> Worse than grizzled piggies.
> My kids are not to blame—
> 'Tis their dad that's guilty.
> As I look at this picture,
> With you loafing all day long,
> I am going to spit, drop it all,
> Will run away, devil take you!"

Nikita Morgunok is shocked at the sight of "triumphant" individualism, but still he clings to his dream. He addresses Stalin (b. 1879) himself, the man who has become a legend, in his lifetime, through the lands of the Union. The Stalin episode is one of Tvardovsky's numerous folk incrustations:

> It grew—at first muffled,
> Spread radio-like—the rumor.
> As an echo through the woods,
> So it ran across the land:
> Stalin is riding, his very self,
> On a raven-black horse.
>
> By waters blue, over hills and fields,
> 'Cross highways and byways,
> In his greatcoat, with his little pipe,
> He rides straight ahead.
> Now he visits one district,
> Now another.
> He looks about, he chats with folks,
> And jots down in his little book
> Every bit right and proper.

Morgunok prepares a speech to Comrade Stalin, in which he pours out all his grievances and aspirations, not forgetting the story of his horse. He does not question the wisdom of destroying the old, nor the advantages of the new order. Only—he would like so much to get the taste of living on his own allotment, with his own horse, if only for a while. Later on he will join the collective, he swears he will. Would not Comrade Stalin do him a favor and issue a decree in that sense, that is, to let Nikita Morgunok remain for the time being an individual holder . . . ?

Tvardovsky pictures thus the average middle-aged peasant about the year 1930, in the early stage of the collectivization process. With his head he accepts the new system as indisputably better than the old one—how can he help seeing that with the aid of mechanized methods collective farming results in better crops than backward individual farming? But his heart still yearns after a Muravia, where every bit is his *own,* where he may stroll about and spit at will. As against Bugrov, the *kulak* type, and Morgunok, the wobbly middler, Tvardovsky draws a portrait of Andrey Frolov, the personification of the new rural element, the collective farmer; his impact on Morgunok has an ultimately decisive effect. Of a powerful physique and strong of will, Frolov has fought all his life against exploiters and oppressors, has known misery and subjection, has been beaten by his enemies almost to death. Now he is a staunch upholder of the new order which frees man from the thralldom of master and property. With Frolov as guide, Morgunok observes the collective farm, its modern machinery, superior crops, growing opulence, and his heart of a soil tiller is thrilled. More than by the tangible signs of well-being, he is impressed by the joviality of these farmers, their geniality and lightness of spirits, the absence of gloom and care and worry which Morgunok has been wont to associate with peasant life. The wedding feast, mentioned previously, sounds a climactic note in this rhapsody of collectivism. The scene ends in Morgunok's recovery of his horse from a fugitive priest who rides up to the feast in the hope of earning a few coins by performing the obsolescent ceremony.

The conversion of Morgunok does not take place then and there. The author continues to mingle realism with fantasy, alternating psychological probability with the whimsicality of a fairy tale. Morgunok, now that his horse is restored to him, leaves the hospitable collective farm and proceeds on his journey to the land of Muravia. After days of travel, he comes upon a venerable ancient dressed as a pilgrim to holy places. The old man admits that he has discovered the futility of pilgrimaging to distant places, when so many good things are taking place so near at home; he is on his way back to his native village. Knocking about a great deal, he has learned that

> "As for God—'tis not exactly that He ain't,
> But He's no longer in power."

Of this man of experience Morgunok inquires for directions to Muravia Land. There is no such place, he is told. Once upon a time there may have existed a Muravia, but it has disappeared, is now overgrown with "grass and sward" (a play on words: *murava* means grass). Who wants this Muravia, anyway, when all around life now is so "handy"? Morgunok gathers that this "handy" land is nowhere but in a collective farm. The author leaves him on the road, ashamed of his long hesitation and fruitless quest, but ready to profit from the wisdom he has acquired:

> "For now I can see all things more clearly
> For thousands of versts around."

Tvardovsky's *Muravia Land* typifies the best of Soviet art today. Though rich and variegated, its form is simple and unobtrusive, finely adapted to the subject; now in iambics, now in singsong amphibrachs. The descriptions are clear and crisp, aptly conveying the very feel of field and soil, yet free from hackneyed epithets and canned lyricism. Above all, the poem meets Tolstoy's first requirement of art—that it be understandable.

The long fight against formalism and naturalism, in behalf of making art appreciable by the huge and exacting Soviet public, has not been in vain. The composer Sergey Prokofyev (b. 1891) has faced in his field the "difficult but interesting problem" encountered by all Soviet artists:

> Music written for the masses must of necessity be simple, but by no means reduced to a repetition of old, worn-out formulas, nor—and that is even more important—must it cater to bad taste.

What Prokofyev has done with folk motifs in his music for *Alexander Nevsky* is suggestive of the way that "difficult but interesting problem" has been solved by Soviet composers and other creative artists. Understandable art does not have to be inferior art; witness the Bible narratives. Tolstoy's latter-day fables and tales, written expressly for the common people, are a high achievement in form and style. Like Prokofyev in music, Tvardovsky and other leading Soviet poets have successfully followed this path of producing work of the highest level, designed not for exclusive circles but for millions of eager and critical readers.

FOLKLORE IN THE MAKING

It is a truism that literacy drives out folklore. Conversely, where illiteracy prevails, one may still come upon oral literature, mostly in verse. The rate of illiteracy has greatly diminished in the Soviet Union, where beside the enforcement of compulsory school attendance by children a vigorous campaign has been carried on for adult education. Still the number of illiterate elderly people remains considerable, especially in remote corners of northern Europe and among the various nationalities of Siberia, Central Asia, and portions of the Caucasus. Out of their midst have come forth in recent years some bards of note, who perform their own compositions, usually to the accompaniment of a native instrument. A number of these bards have displayed extraordinary talent and originality, and have won the acclaim of the public and the critics as well as recognition, decorations, and awards from local and central authorities. As is natural for folk literature, a large quantity of songs and tales circulates anonymously, now as an Uzbek shepherd song, now as a Kalmuck collective-farm parable or story, or a Buryat-Mongol lay, or a Swanetia hunting song. Most of these folk creations, whether anonymous or of known authorship, belong to heroic epos describing the exploits of Soviet men and women who have distinguished themselves in one way or another, whether as warriors, or as statesmen, aviators, explorers, shock workers, and the like. As might be expected, the man who has caught the fancy of most of the folk poets is Lenin, with Stalin following in popularity. The singers use traditional form, stock epithets, hyperboles, and they do not hesitate to introduce supernatural forces even when they adhere to factual substance.

True to its policy of fostering cultural expressions in the hundred-and-fifty-odd linguistic varieties of the Union, the Moscow authorities have given aid and courage to creators and disseminators of folk poetry. Aside from the recognition of individual artists in this field, an attempt has been made at organizing them as a collective group. In the summer of 1939 a conference of folk singers and reciters from all over the Union was held in Moscow. Most of them were old men and women who have preserved the ancient technique of popular song and tale traditionally intact. There was only a small nucleus of original composers, from among the Russian people and national minorities, who were inspired by the old lore to apply its forms to contemporary subjects. The singers and reciters, nearly all of them from the backwoods, were dazzled by the splendor of the capital and deeply moved by the hospitality and admiration they received from the authorities and from academic and artistic groups. At the conference they discussed regional and national problems, and adopted suitable measures to guard folk riches, to cherish the heritage, and to further and expand it.

Marfa Kryukova.—Of the epic singers of Russia proper, mention must be made especially of Marfa Kryukova (b. 1876), who has spent nearly all the seven decades of her life in the north, by the White Sea. Remoteness from centers of civilization in part explains why that region is rich in folklore. Marfa Kryukova comes from a family of reciters, *skaziteli,* who have kept up the tradition of *byliny*-chanters for generations, definitely from the time of Peter the Great. Marfa possesses a fine memory, her repertory exceeding one hundred and fifty items. Though illiterate, she has a wide knowledge of Russian history, past and present, and a keen if at times oversimplified understanding of national and international issues. So steeped is she in the old lore that in ordinary conversation she is apt to revert to epic style and improvise in the *byliny* manner. Some of these improvisations have been written down in late years, and a few have been published. Of her three best known "recitations" (*skazaniya*), one deals with Lenin, another with the celebrated civil war hero, Chapayev (1887–1919), and the third describes the Arctic expedition of Otto Schmidt (b. 1891), and the rescue of himself and his crew by Soviet fliers. She has the gift of clothing current events in ancient garb and lending them the charm of the old and the fanciful. Thus, the story of long-whiskered Schmidt, stranded on an ice floe, and of the valiant aviators is given under the title: *Beard-to-the-Knee and the Bright Falcons* (*Pokolyen-Boroda i yasnyie sokoly*). Chapayev (Kryukova calls him, colloquilly, Chapay) becomes a golden-winged eagle flying over the glorious Volga steppes. Her greatest skill in blending modernity of theme with archaic solemnity is shown in her *Lay of Lenin*.

Marfa Kryukova gives an account of the important events in Lenin's life, coloring them in conventional *bylina* hues, but hardly ever distorting the essential historical truth. She begins her tale with the attempt of Lenin's elder brother, Alexander (1866–1887), against the life of Tsar Alexander III (1845–1894). The opening lines ring with the majesty of stock parallelisms:

> In those days, in former ones,
> In those times, in olden ones,
> Under Big-Idol Tsar of foul memory,
> In Simbirsk, fine city on Volga River . . .

Alexander's attempt to free the people from the tsar, his failure, and his execution are narrated in grand style. On hearing of his death, the mother tears her white hair and sheds "hot tears" down the steep river bank, so that "from her tears the Volga water grows turgid." She calls on her children "to stand for their brother, to fight for beloved brother Sashenka, for his truth, the people's truth." The answer of her son Vladimir (Lenin) is a curious mixture of fairy-tale elements with such actualities as his Marxian

preparation or his opposition to individual terrorism as impractical
romanticism:

> "Grieve not, mother dear, do not sorrow.
> We will, indeed, take a great vow amongst us,
> A great vow for people's truth to battle!
> Wet not, loved mother, thy fair face,
> Do not spoil thy bright eyes.
> For I feel in me a great power:
> Were that ring in an oaken pillar,
> I'd wrench it out, myself with my comrades,
> With that faithful bodyguard of mine—
> I'd then turn about the whole damp mother earth!
> Well am I trained in wise learning,
> For I've read one magic little book,
> Now I know where to find the ring,
> Now I know how to turn about the whole earth,
> The whole earth, our whole dear Russia.
> Give leave, dear mother, for me to start my journey-road,
> Through cities I shall go, and cross many seas,
> I shall see-behold all the people,
> I must gather a great force—
> For to go forth and seek out that wonder ring,
> With that ring we shall turn the whole damp earth,
> Turn to the right side, the just one.
> That will not be the honor of a man of prowess,
> Nor a knight's glorious fame:
> To kill a tsar is a small gain,
> One you kill, another tsar mounts.
> We must, we must fight in another way—
> Against all princes, against the nobles all,
> Against the whole up-to-now order!"

Thus mingling fact and fancy, Kryukova proceeds to describe
Lenin's efforts to gather together "peasants, tillers of the soil," factory workers, and "learned men," to form a "great people's force"
for "wresting the wonder ring" (a well-known folk motif) and
for the abolition of the "injustice of rich men." Arrested and exiled
to Siberia, Lenin warms his benumbed fingers by a bonfire, and in

its light he writes "express letters," and sends them out to "all lands," instructing the people how to carry on the struggle. Deviating from history, Kryukova has a symbolic Ivan, a Siberian "not well-to-do *muzhik*," help Lenin escape abroad. In a foreign town, "free from tsars and kings," he sits by a table and continues to write "express letters" on "how to fight against tsars and 'bourzhuys.' " One night he hears a knock on the window; cautiously he opens the "oaken door," and beholds a fair maiden named Nadezhda, daughter of Konstantin (Krupskaya). She has escaped from a Russian jail and has come to join him, to be to him a "helpmate, a helpmate and partaker, to be a faithful wife, a faithful and unchanging wife."

Ivan, the Siberian *muzhik,* advises Lenin of the Bloody Sunday (January 22, 1905). In substance the event is described correctly in a simplified version of the "villainy" of the tsar, of his uncle the Grand Duke Vladimir (1847–1909), and the perfidious priest Gapon (1870–1906). Lenin takes leave of his wife, mounts a snow-white horse with a black mane and tail, and after many days and nights he reaches the Moscow Sparrow Hills (now Lenin Hills). In the poem these hillocks become "steep mountains, famous Sparrow Mountains." From their peak Lenin watches his poor country, sees heads rolling in the streets, people dragged to prison, exiled, shot, and "all Russia cowed."

Later the war breaks out. "Sly and cunning Yermania" desires to take possession of the lands of Russia. The tsar mobilizes countless armies and sends them down to "deep marshes" and up to high mountains, "higher than coursing clouds." But there is treason in the rear. While Tsar "Nikolasha" (Nicholas II, 1868–1918) drinks and brags, his wife reveals all military secrets to the Kaiser, who addresses her as his "blood-kindred niece." This is fiction, of course, as is the item recounting how one of her traitorous letters falls into the hands of Russian soldiers. These are "terrified"; they reckon that "things are bad, bad and unbearable," and resolve to bring an

end to the war, "not to shed their blood in vain." The overthrow of
the monarchy, the arrival of Lenin, his speeches, his flight from
Kerensky's police, his hiding place in a "little tent," disguised as
a "little shepherd," are described with ingenuous charm. The October revolution assumes a fairy-tale aspect:

> On a morning it was, on an early morning,
> At the rise of the fair red sun,
> That Ilich[6] stepped out of his little tent,
> He washed his fair face
> With spring water cold,
> His face he wiped with a little towel.
> As he played on his birchbark horn,
> The whole people heard him,
> The whole people gathered and thronged.
> They all thronged and gathered,
> Up to that pillar the marvelous.
> They gathered in a mighty force,
> They took hold on the little ring, the magic one,
> Hard it was to wrench the little ring,
> With stout force they did wrench it,
> Turned about glorious mother Russia land,
> To another side, the just one,
> And took away the keys of little Russia
> From those landlords, from factory owners.

The triumphant people entrust Lenin with the "golden keys of
the whole land." Lenin proceeds to appoint "friend Stalin as an
aid," he "takes into service men of common birth, of common birth
and from among the poor," and it goes without saying that he
appoints Ivan, the Siberian *muzhik*, a people's commissar. Kryukova enumerates some of Lenin's achievements, such as the termination of the war and the nationalization of land, commerce, and
industry. The people rejoiced and "sang merry songs in content-
ment"—but not for long. "A dark stormcloud rose over the land,
over Soviet little Russia.... Generals and constables, landlords and

---

[6] Familiar appellation of Lenin, for Vladimir Ilich Ulyanov.

factory owners, princes and nobles, merchants, exceeding wealthy ones" gathered together to conspire against the new order. The civil war was on. Alarmed by the attack of "ferocious lions and infamous dogs," Lenin summons out of the vast steppes "Klim the locksmith, glorious Voroshilov" (b. 1881), and the "heroic Red Cossack Budenny from the quiet Don." These are joined by the troops of Vasily "Chapay" and "valiant Blücher" (b. 1889). The White armies then "swayed, they shook and they quaked," and their generals appealed for help to "foreign kings." Help was proffered by these "with full pleasure": they desired to see a tsar reign over Russia, "they desired therefor to receive costly gifts"—Russian lands.

At this "troubled time" Lenin was wounded by a counterrevolutionary: "A fierce snake glided up, she stung, she struck leader-Lenin, barely missed his dear little heart, but she made a wound and a very deep one, the evildoer, a very deep and poisonous one." Lenin's wife sent for famous healers,

> Herself she ran forth from the chamber,
> She ran straight to the garden green,
> She plucked grass weeds,
> Plucked green leaves of every kind,
> Gathered and brought them in,
> And laid them on the hot little wound.

On regaining consciousness, the wounded leader summons Stalin and urges him to go forth to the Red army and rouse its courage "with his valiant strength and with his wise counsel." Stalin comes before the warriors, "rises in the stirrups," and makes a speech in the *byliny* style:

> "Hey you fellows soldiers of the Red Army,
> Hey you famous factory workers,
> Hey you peasants, black-soil tillers:
> A time has come, a most hard one,
> A time has come, a most warlike one.
> We must gather our last strength,

> With our valorous valor must we crush the enemies,
> Crush the enemies, scatter all evildoers.
> Vladimir Ilich has sent me to you,
> He is sick abed and moaning,
> On account of the evil snake, of the deep wound:
> Let us crush the enemy, then he'll get well!"

Needless to say, Stalin's speech has the desired effect. The Red troops hurled themselves against the enemies, broke their ranks, pursued them day and night, and

> Into the blue seas they cast all the yenerals:[7]
> One yeneral with his army into our own White Sea,
> Another yeneral with his army into that Black Sea,
> A third yeneral with his army into that Western Sea [the Baltic],
> A fourth yeneral with his army into the Far-East Sea.
> All other yenerals with their colonels,
> With the colonels and with the majors,
> They drove into miry swamps,
> And into deep rivers, rapid ones,
> And there they met their end.

All is well now with the Soviet lands, the peoples rejoice, and Lenin seems to be on the way to recovery. But—and here Marfa Kryukova scorns chronology and facts—the treasonable actions of Trotsky disturb Lenin's mind and aggravate his illness. The leader is dying. He bids farewell to Nadezhda Konstantinovna, "his faithful helpmate, faithful and unchanging one," and he hands over the golden keys of the land to Stalin, "his dear and true friend." The death of Lenin is recorded in the conventional *byliny* images:

> It was not the fair sun has rolled
> Beyond those famous Sparrow Mountains,
> Nor beyond mother stonewall-Moscow,
> Nor again beyond those dark forests,
> Nor beyond those orchards, all green,

---

[7] The reciter uses an archaic pronunciation of the word "general."

Nor beyond those seas did it set, the deep ones,
Nor beyond those cities, all the different ones,
Nor beyond the villages and little hamlets,
Nor beyond creeks, quiet ones:
Our fair sun has rolled down,
Moreover the moon from beneath the sky,
Moreover the dawn, the morning dawn,
Moreover the star, the evening star.
Our fair sun has rolled down,
When into mother, into damp earth,
When into the grave was laid,
Was laid, indeed, Ilich our light,
And covered with coffin boards.
Birds flew up then like falcons high to the skies,
Fishes then sank to the deep of the seas,
Foxes-martens scampered over the islands,
Friend-bears scattered through the dark woods,
And people put on black clothes,
Black clothes they put on, sorrowful clothes.
To his grave they all thronged,
Thronged all and came together—
Muzhiks those village folk,
Workers all from factories,
Workers all of Soviet learning,
No number and counting to all that came.
Then all peoples burst weeping,
In different voices of different tribes—
The whole dear earth was drenched with hot tears. . . .

Amidst the lamentation of all peoples, Stalin proclaims the celebrated oath of loyalty to Lenin and his beliefs. The poem ends with
a curious touch about the Lenin mausoleum on the Red Square,
made, according to Kryukova's ornamental whim, out of precious
stones:

Those stones all peoples carried up,
Each people brought one stone apiece.
And the peoples put up a little house of death,
Therein lies Ilich, sleeps in peace.

THE POETS AND THE WAR

On June 22, 1941, Hitler's troops invaded Soviet territory. Though they had expected this inevitable clash and were not unprepared for it, the Soviet people were somewhat stunned by the perfidy of the recent co-signatory to the nonaggression pact. The arts were silenced for the moment. The general feeling was that the fighting front needed everyone, and everything was to be dedicated to that front.

Very soon, however, it became clear that in this total war all creative forces had to be mobilized. The fighting front and the productive front demanded copious and adequate food and equipment, intellectual and artistic as well as material. Olga Knipper, the widow of Anton Chekhov, observed the keen response of war audiences to the arts, a response matching the eagerness of artists to serve the war. To quote from her statement:

"We do not need poetry," say the Germans, "we need guns." Well, *we* need poetry too. Our poetry is also "at the front." The genuine poet is aware today of the one possible happiness—to live the lot of his country. No matter how much the Fascist obscurantists try to lower man, to convert him into an automaton, a machine, a slave, their efforts will prove vain. Man—that has a proud sound [Gorky's words. A. K.]. With bullet, with bayonet, with verse, with all our great art we shall defend the beautiful realm of proud man—our country, our motherland.

The need of poetry in time of war was manifested quite early, when the defenders of Voronezh demanded a supply of the collected verse of two Voronezh folk poets, A. V. Koltsov (1809–1842) and Ivan Nikitin (1824–1861). Living poets came to the front, along with musicians, actors, dancers, to share the life of the soldiers, to entertain and to create. The delicate lyricist Yosif Utkin lost his fingers, shot off by German shrapnel, and, no longer able to write, dictated lines of hate from his hospital cot. On all fronts, from the Arctic to the Black Sea and the Caucasus, and in all the besieged cities, from Leningrad and Moscow to Sevastopol and Stalingrad, the voice of the poet regularly mingled with the sounds of bursting shells and droning planes.

The attitude of the poet to the present war is succinctly expressed by Nikolay Tikhonov, who had sensed the world catastrophe in prose and verse decades before it broke forth. To him,

this is not an ordinary war that ends in discussions at a peace conference about two or three provinces and several carloads of gold indemnity. No, the destiny of mankind is involved, the question of what kind of world will emerge from under the ruins, of what man will do and how he will live on this earth, and first of all how the Soviet man will live on Soviet earth.

Tikhonov tells us how after the momentary silence, the "terrible pause," art regained its voice:

With every day of the war men of art revived. It became clear that the muses cannot be silent. The witnesses of terrible days began to speak in the language of literature, painting, music, without waiting for the days to come. They began to speak today. The war, our motherland, love for freedom, revenge—these have begun to live in prose and in poetry. A new front has been created, the front of art, and it is broadening apace....

If the Fascists are burning books, we shall proceed to write new ones. If the Fascists write books full of savagery and darkness, we shall burn them with the fire of satire. If the band of Goebbels-Rosenberg-Hitler is howling about man the murderer, man the beast, as the ornament of future society, we shall tell of man of good will, and of the most terrible force—justice; if the Fascists are impelled to glorify the slavery of all nations except the German, we shall write about the freedom of all nations; if they have debased woman to the lowest degree, we shall write verses and songs about the grandeur of our women, about youth and beauty.

Spring is on her way. The ice is breaking, the snow darkens, the day grows brighter.... We welcome spring. She will not save the Germans. Let them not place their hope in clear, bright weather: in all events they are men of darkness. At their own risk they have invoked the ancient myth about the battle of darkness and light. This conflict has been decided long ago. As long as there is a sun in the skies, it will remain invincible. Under its dynamic fire, night retreats day after day. Thus it has been from time immemorial; thus it shall be even now. We are marching to meet spring with arms and song. In our music and in the thunder of our cannon we hear one and the same flaming word: victory. To it we have given our heart and our inspiration.

The war has stimulated a revival of the "old" poets, and has brought forth a crop of new ones. The acmeist Akhmatova has broken her long silence. Even the veteran Demyan Bedny has reappeared on the pages of dailies and weeklies with his facile verse. At the other extreme, David Burlyuk has been singing patriotic verses in good clear iambics (in the New York daily, *Russky golos*). Boris Pasternak has published some polished war lyrics, though his main output is still in the field of translations. Among his recent achievements one should mention poems from the Polish romanticist, Julius Slowacki, and his masterly *Romeo and Juliet,* which excels even his *Hamlet* in approaching the sparkling simplicity of Shakespeare. Alexander Bezymensky has continued his march from Mayakovsky back to Pushkin, both in form and content; he has written some notable war verses in regular meter. There has been an outburst of songs, lyrics, and ballads on war themes by such of the men discussed in the foregoing pages as Lebedev-Kumach, Mikhalkov, Kirsanov, Utkin, Golodny, Gusev, Svetlov, Zharov, and a number of younger poets, like Isakovsky, Shchipachev, Yashin, Dolmatovsky, whose names were hardly known before 1941. Except for Kirsanov, who still retains certain futuristic mannerisms, the Soviet poets have definitely freed themselves from the fetters of formalism. What they have to say is usually strikingly fresh and devoid of clichés, yet clearly understandable. Such is the virtue of the average Soviet poet, the net result of years of struggle and verbal warfare.

A survey of Soviet poetry since the latter part of 1941 might fill another volume. I should like to mention here only a few of the more notable contributions to war poetry, by way of supplementing the preceding chapters.

Tvardovsky, author of *Muravia Land,* has been quite prolific in his short pieces. Most of them are in ballad form, depicting war episodes, particularly bits of guerrilla warfare. Only one of his poems approaches *Muravia Land* in scope and mastery, *Vasily Tyorkin.* Here Tvardovsky attempts a generic Russian soldier, or, more correctly, a Soviet soldier. Vasily Tyorkin typifies the homely wisdom of the average Russian man of the masses, his rhythmic speech, the dexterity of his hands, and his inventiveness in moments of trial and crisis. At the same time, he is a typical Soviet citizen in the brand of patriotism that motivates his actions. Unlike Tolstoy's Platon Karatayev, and unlike Nekrasov's peasants whom he resembles in his colorful speech, Tyorkin is imbued with the dignity of citizenship, with the pride of a patriotism based on reason and knowledge of what one owes to one's country and its social order. The poem is written in a humorous tone that does not change even in grave moments. Tvardovsky displays his deepening understanding of the common people and of their rich language. Yet the poem falls short of *Muravia Land* in lacking the continuity of growth that we witness in the adventures of Nikita Morgunok. *Vasily Tyorkin* is a series of episodes, some of them epic in quality and diapason; but the hero, so far as his traits and views are concerned, remains static throughout.

The poem is, quite naturally, a favorite with the fighting men. A number of Leningrad poets, professional and amateur, recently published a collection of verses on the new adventures of Tyorkin, *Vasily Tyorkin on the Leningrad Front,* illustrated by Boris Leo. Apparently Tyorkin is becoming a folk hero, inviting imitation and expansion.

A good deal of war poetry is related to guerrilla fighting, which expresses the most heroic and most folklike aspect of the war. Nearly all the best poets have dealt with this thrilling theme. Svetlov, Surkov, Dolmatovsky, Antokolsky, and many others have repeatedly presented, with reserved emotionalism, such dramatic

features of guerrilla warfare as small boys and girls performing
dangerous services as scouts or grenade throwers. The poet has to
beware of the pitfall of melodrama, he must be suggestive rather
than outspoken in depicting such raw tragedy, and furthermore,
in presenting these heroic exploits, which are taking place on a
mass scale, he faces the task of portraying a collective phenomenon
without effacing the individual. Soviet poets have coped with this
problem admirably. You are aware of their pent-up emotion, the
spasm in the throat, the burning anger at the sadistic degenerates,
violators, and murderers of children, but all this is held under re-
straint and noble reserve. The poetess Margarita Aliger has written
a long narrative poem, *Zoya,* in which she describes the life and
death of the ninth-grade schoolgirl, Zoya Kosmodemyanskaya.
This girl, whom the Germans tortured, lashed, and finally hanged,
failing to break her spirit, has become well-nigh a legend in the
Soviet Union. Margarita Aliger was not afraid of treating so dangerously popular and immediate a subject. Her poem has the dignity and perspective of an epic.

Two members of the short-lived but boisterous school of constructivists, Selvinsky and Inber, have gained prominence with
their war poems. Selvinsky's fine gift of producing a vivid image
by means of carefully selected concrete details has served him well
at the various battlefronts. He makes you visualize the madness
and horror which he has personally observed and lived through,
and he does it in unpretentious iambics, with incisive nouns and
verbs, very few adjectives, and hardly any metaphors. One of his
poems has the characteristic title: "I Saw This Myself." The virtually indescribable horror of heaps of corpses, victims of German
sadistic ingenuity, is suggested by a few apposite details that etch
themselves in one's mind and memory indelibly.

Vera Inber has immortalized Leningrad, whose siege she has
lived through to tell us of the sufferings and heroism of the inhabi-
tants. Most notable among her many writings on this theme is her

long poem *Pulkovo meridian,* composed in the form of a diary. Its
stark directness is suggested by the title of one chapter, "Light and
Warmth," in which she speaks of the privations suffered by the
besieged. The poet muses and daydreams (of a brown crust of rye
bread), as she lies in bed gloved and booted, under two fur coats,
a kerchief protecting her head. No electricity, no fuel, no food, and
even the water pipes are out of order, so that the citizens make
their way to the Neva River and stand in line with buckets in front
of an ice hole. In a conversational tone Inber observes the effects of
the regime on its victims:

> ... From day to day
> The calcium in our cells grows less and less
> And we grow weaker. Take me, now. Some way,
> I scratched my finger in my carelessness.
> That's three months back, as near as I can tell,
> And yet, devil take it, it will not get well.
>
> How painfully—still worse, how swiftly—can
> Faces grow old these days! The features stand
> Out, cut to birdlike sharpness by the hand,
> It seems, of some ill-omened make-up man.
> A pinch of ashes and a little lead—
> And faces look like faces of the dead.
>
> The teeth are bared, the mouth drawn tight, the face
> Is waxen and the beard like a cadaver's
> (A beard the razor hardly can displace).
> The walk, without a balance center, wavers.
> The pulse beneath the ashen-colored skin
> Is weak. The albumin is gone. The end sets in.
>
> Among the women many have a swelling.
> They shiver constantly (though not from frost).
> Their bosoms shrink to nothingness, compelling
> The once white kerchiefs to be tighter crossed.
> Who would believe that once at such a breast
> A child had ever sucked himself to rest?

Like melted candles in their apathy.
All the dry summaries and indications
Are here of what by learned designations
Doctors call "alimental dystrophy."
Non-Latinists, nonphilologues, will name
It simply hunger, but it means the same.

And after that the end is very near.
The body, rolled up in a dust-gray cover
Fastened with safety pins, and wound all over
With rope, upon a child's sled will appear,
So neatly laid out that it's plain to see
It's not the first one in the family.[8]

These experiences amid scenes of "luxuriating winter" do not dampen, however, the fire of loyalty to the cause, nor the flaming hatred for the "Hitlerite delirium." Vera Inber has poured into her poem the noble tragedy of a people ready to suffer and die so that the life they love may not be extinguished by mechanized brutality.

The tragic days of Leningrad have thus far fared in art better than any other episode in the present war, the siege of Stalingrad not excepted. No one has as yet excelled Shostakovich's Seventh symphony as a monumental expression of the spirit of Leningrad. Among the numerous literary contributions to this theme, one must note, besides the Inber poem, at least one other worthy endeavor, the verses of Nikolay Tikhonov. In prose and verse, in articles and speeches, Tikhonov has paid homage to the city he loves and to the unbreakable will to freedom of its citizens. I believe that one may get an idea of the role of the poet in wartime Russia by reading an extract from a paper by Alexander Fadeyev, President of the Writers' Union, which I translate:

The workers of the Kirov plant requested us to arrange for them a literary evening. On the program were the Leningrad poets, Nikolay Tikhonov, Alexander Prokofyev, and myself.

In the basement of one of the buildings, underneath a cemented floor,

---

[8] Dorothea Prall Radin is the co-translator of these lines.

they have arranged a hall for meetings and entertainments, with a stage and scenery. The hall, with seats for several hundred people, was overfilled. All passages were crowded, and they had to lock the entrance door. All through the evening, people tried to break in, although just then artillery began shelling the plant.

Nikolay Tikhonov read his poem *Kirov Is with Us*. The subject of the poem is how Kirov, the late leader and favorite of Leningrad workers, goes the rounds of blockaded Leningrad on a cold black iron night.

The power of this superb poem was enhanced by the fact that Tikhonov wrote it during the current cruel winter, in his unheated rooms, by the light of a little kerosene lamp, and by the fact that he himself was reading it to the Kirov workers, in the basement of one of the Kirov plant buildings, during a heavy artillery shelling of the plant. All listened to the poem as though petrified. The faces of the listeners were severe and touching.

There is a chapter in the poem in which Kirov passes by the plant that bears his name:

> Buildings are smashed, and fences;
> The ruined vaults gape wide.
> In the iron nights of Leningrad
> Kirov goes through the city;
> That just and terrible warrior
> Quietly goes through the city.
> The hour is late, deep and cold.
> Austere, like a fortress, is the plant.
> Here, there is no pause in the work;
> Here, rest is forgotten, and sleep;
> Here, men by a great care are weighed down,
> Drops of sweat on their temples.
> What if the red flame of a shell
> Has more than once crimsoned the shops!
> Work conscientiously, properly.
> Banish fatigue and fear.
> Momentary languor may grip
> The men, but lo, an old man comes forth.
> Hear what this grandfather will say;
> His tongue is incorruptible.
> "What if our soup is watery?
> What if bread is priced like gold?

> We will stand firm like steel:
> There will be time to get tired later on.
> The enemy could not break us by force,
> So he wants to take us by hunger,
> To grab Leningrad from Russia,
> The Leningraders to imprison.
> This shall never, never take place
> On the sacred shores of the Neva.
> Our workers are Russian men;
> They will die but not yield to the enemy.
> We shall forge new arms for the front,
> We will break the enemy's ring.
> Not for nothing is our severe plant
> Proudly named after Kirov.

While Tikhonov read these lines tears rolled down the brave faces of the Kirov workers, both men and women. Tikhonov himself was moved. When he finished, he received an ovation, and was called out again and again.

The relations between the front and the poets may be illustrated by the tank "Ruthless." Four poets, Gusev, Marshak, Mikhalkov, and Tikhonov, and three painters, known by the collective name of Kukriniksi, all of whom were awarded the Stalin prize (100,000 to 200,000 rubles), converted their prizes into a tank which they named "Ruthless." The Kukriniksi painted on either side of the tank a gay cartoon with verses by Marshak and Mikhalkov:

> Carry on your fiery attack,
> O heavy tank of ours!
> Get behind the fascist rear,
> Knock him on the flank!
> Your fearless crew,
> Ever wakeful and alert,
> Is carrying out
> Stalin's war order.

In a reduced size the cartoon and the verses were engraved on a brass plate and placed inside the tank by the commander's seat.

Three months later the laureates received a letter from the officers of the tank, reporting on their exploits in a number of battles against the enemy. The officers and crew were proud of their tank and of the dedication, which inspired them to acts of fearless courage. The letter ended with the assuring lines: "At the present time, 'Ruthless' is in the rank of active machines and, proceeding to batter the fascist filth, it is executing to perfection the task assigned by you." Incidentally, the close coöperation of artists and poets in war-posters and billboards has proved extremely effective for the morale of the army and civilians.

In the growing volume of lyrics the prevailing motive is dual: love and hatred. Antokolsky, Svetlov, Dolmatovsky, and numerous others interweave their sentiments with this woof and warp. It seems inevitable that tenderness for one's mother and child should invoke implacable vengeance against their tormentors and murderers, that love for one's land and its way of living should spell unreserved hatred for the invader whose victory means slavery. This dichotomy is voiced by Alexey Surkov:

> In the night we had faith in the dawn
> That shall rise out of blood.
> We knew that without wrath can be
> Neither happiness nor love.
> And in the rare hour when
> We managed to get some wine,
> We drained the glass at a gulp
> To hatred and anger.
> A heavy road is given us,
> But forge thou a lasting song—
> The time will come to raise a toast
> To brotherhood and love.

Soviet patriotism has forged a new loyalty to the fatherland, to its history and traditions. Words and conceptions that were hated through their association with the oppressive past have now assumed a new significance and value. The poet no longer hesitates to speak without malice of "soldier," "general," "church," "sacred soil." It is symptomatic that the theme of personal love sounds more and more frequently in war lyrics. By invoking the image of his beloved the warrior draws strength for his national love-hate sentiment. Best known of these poems is one by Konstantin Simonov, "Wait for Me," which is recited and sung from one end of the country to the other, and has recently been expanded into a play and produced with great success. Young Simonov is both prolific and versatile. To American audiences he is known for his play *The Russian People.* "Wait for Me" is a fragment from a long, as yet unfinished, cycle under the title *With You and without You.* Simonov has seen much during this war, serving as a correspondent on many fronts. In his cycle he records his impressions and moods, invariably linking them with a yearning for his beloved. The fragment that has become popular is not his best verse, but is typical of Simonov's whimsical muse:

> Wait for me and I'll come back,
> But wait with might and main.
> Wait throughout the gloom and rack
> Of autumn's yellow rain.
> Wait when snowstorms fill the way,
> Wait in summer's heat,
> Wait when, false to yesterday,
> Others do not wait.
> Wait when from afar at last
> No letters come to you.
> Wait when all the rest have ceased
> To wait, who waited too.
>
> Wait for me and I'll come back.
> Do not lightly let
> Those, who know so well the knack,
> Teach you to forget.
> Let my mother and my son
> Believe that I have died;
> Let my friends, with waiting done,

At the fireside
Lift the wine of grief and clink
To my departed soul.
Wait, and make no haste to drink,
Alone amongst them all.

Wait for me and I'll come back,
Defying death. When he
Who could not wait shall call it luck
Only, let it be.
They cannot know, who did not wait,
How in the midst of fire
Your waiting saved me from my fate,
Your waiting and desire.
Why I still am living, we
Shall know, just I and you:
You knew how to wait for me
As no other knew.[9]

The revolution of 1917 has upset the apathetic existence of millions and millions of Russian and non-Russian masses on the vast territory of the former empire. They were jolted out of passivity and mute submission and forced to act and think and speak for themselves. The expression of this change, in the arts, has required time to progress from the hysterical pandemonium of the early days. In poetry we have noted the groping efforts, the exaggerations and eccentricities, the confusion of tongues and styles, the whole commotion of growing pains. Not all the battles recorded in this essay were futile or sterile; many of them helped clear the soil for a fruitful and healthy growth. The extraordinary experiences of the last twenty-five years, the spirit of creative reciprocity among the motley nationalities of the Union, and the sense of security and confidence in the future that imbues the citizens of the young state and fires them with heroic zeal in defending it, augur well for the emergence and development of a literature worthy of its nineteenth-century pioneers and masters.

[9] Translated by Dorothea Prall Radin.

Index